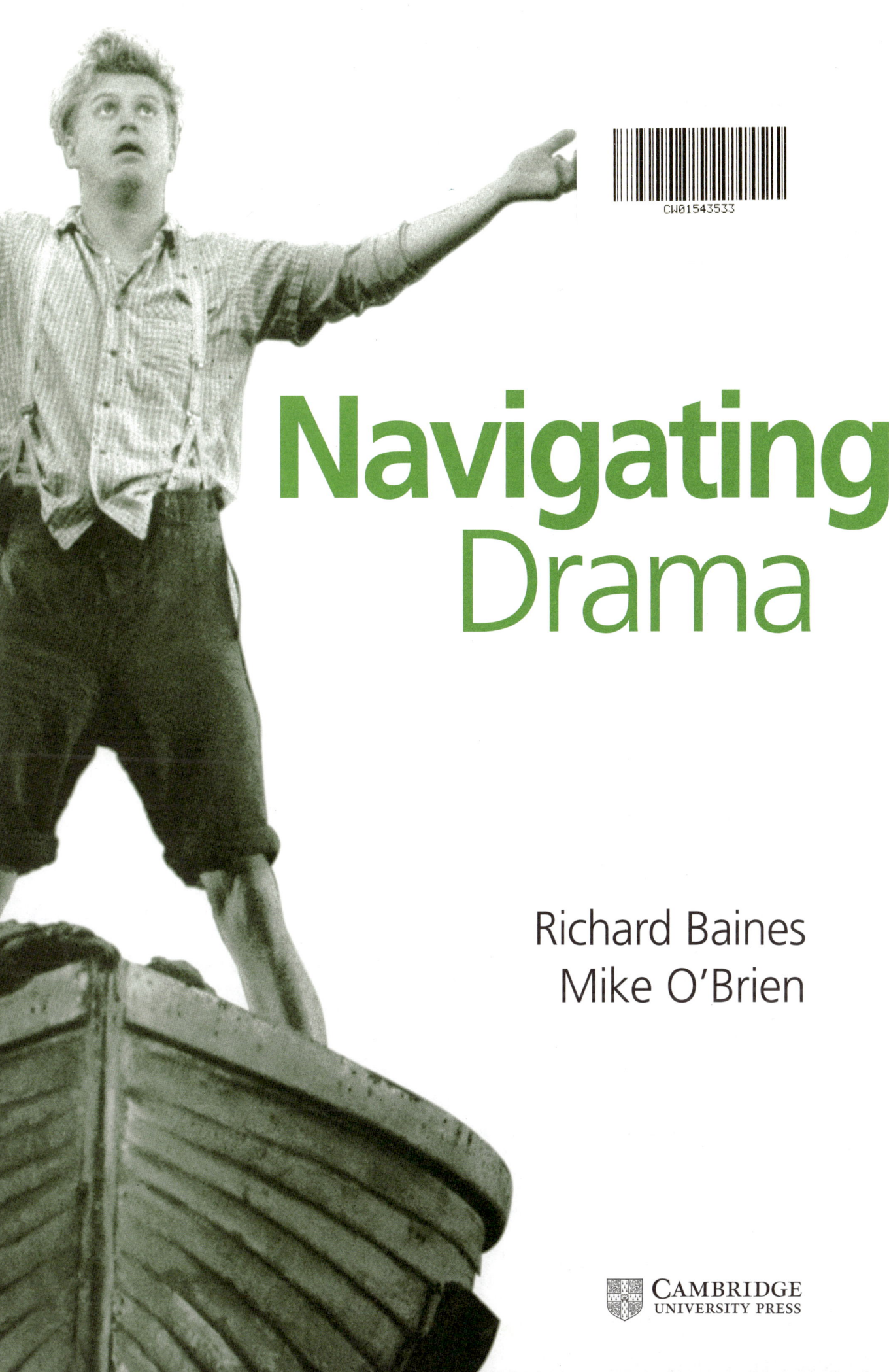

Navigating Drama

Richard Baines
Mike O'Brien

CAMBRIDGE UNIVERSITY PRESS

CAMBRIDGE UNIVERSITY PRESS
Cambridge, New York, Melbourne, Madrid, Cape Town, Singapore, São Paulo

Cambridge University Press
477 Williamstown Road, Port Melbourne, VIC 3207, Australia

www.cambridge.edu.au
Information on this title: www.cambridge.edu.au/0521606187

© Richard Baines and Mike O' Brien 2005

First published 2005
Reprinted 2006, 2008

Printed in Australia by BPA Print Group

National Library of Australia Cataloguing in Publication data
    Baines, Richard, 1941- .
    Navigating drama.
    Includes index.
    ISBN 0 521 60618 7.
Drama–Textbooks. 2. Acting–Textbooks. I. O'Brien,
    Mike. II. Title.
792.02

ISBN-13: 9780521606189 paperback
ISBN-0 521 60618 7 paperback

Reproduction and Communication for educational purposes
The Australian *Copyright Act 1968* (the Act) allows a maximum of
one chapter or 10% of the pages of this work, whichever is the greater,
to be reproduced and/or communicated by any educational institution
for its educational purposes provided that the educational institution
(or the body that administers it) has given a remuneration notice to
Copyright Agency Limited (CAL) under the Act.

For details of the CAL licence for educational institutions contact:

Copyright Agency Limited
Level 19, 157 Liverpool Street
Sydney NSW 2000
Telephone: (02) 9394 7600
Facsimile: (02) 9394 7601
E-mail: info@copyright.com.au

Reproduction and Communication for other purposes
Except as permitted under the Act (for example a fair dealing for the
purposes of study, research, criticism or review) no part of this work
may be reproduced, stored in a retrieval system, communicated or
transmitted in any form or by any means without prior written permission.
All inquiries should be made to the publisher at the address above.

Cambridge University Press has no responsibility for
the persistence or accuracy of URLs for external or
third-party internet websites referred to in this work
and does not guarantee that any content on such
websites is, or will remain, accurate or appropriate.

Contents

Introduction
    The elements of *Navigating Drama*   v
    How to use the logbook   vi

Part One: Playbuilding

Chapter 1 Starting the journey   3
    Improvisation   4
    The elements of drama   9
    Spontaneous improvisation   11
    Role   16
    Status   19
    Conflict   21
    Planned improvisation   22
    Unit assessment Making and performing drama: A planned improvisation   26

Chapter 2 Navigating playbuilding   29
    Playbuilding   30
    Narrative playbuilding   34
    Unit assessment Making and performing drama: Narrative playbuilding   41
    Collage playbuilding   43
    Unit assessment Making and performing drama: Collage playbuilding   46
    Issue-based playbuilding   48
    Unit assessment Making and performing drama: Issue-based playbuilding   53

Part Two: Dramatic contexts

Chapter 3 Commedia dell'Arte   57
    Background   58
    The elements of *Commedia*   59
    The script   77
    Unit assessment Performing drama: Performing a *Commedia* scene   82

Chapter 4 Melodrama   85
    The elements of melodrama   86
    The theatres   94
    The plays   96
    The audience   103
    Australian melodrama   104
    Unit assessment Performing melodrama: The Sunny South   110

Chapter 5 Scripted drama – scenes · 113

    What is a script? · 114
    Choosing a script · 114
    Blocking · 128
    Working with a script · 132
    Unit assessment Performing drama: Performing scripted drama · 137

Chapter 6 Scripted drama – monologues · 139

    Choosing a monologue · 140
    Performing a monologue · 147
    Unit assessment Performing drama: Developing and performing a monologue · 158

Chapter 7 Scriptwriting · 161

    What is a script? · 162
    Tricks of the trade · 167
    Structuring the scene · 177
    Unit assessment Making drama: Writing your own scene · 183

Glossary · 185

Index · 191

Acknowledgements · 197

The elements of Navigating Drama

Navigating Drama is in two parts: *Playbuilding* and *Dramatic contexts*.

Part 1 Playbuilding

The *Playbuilding* part of the book provides exercises, games and techniques which will help students of any age develop their improvisation skills. It is a guide to the development and performing of an original piece of theatre. Playbuilding develops a range of creative and performance skills and is a core part of the syllabus.

Part 2 Dramatic contexts

The *Dramatic contexts* part of the book provides a choice of topics for drama students to study in depth.

The book includes a range of practical tasks to allow students to apply and expand their experience. These can be found throughout each chapter as 'Stagecraft', 'On your Feet' and 'Unit Assessment' features.

Stagecraft

Stagecraft tasks provide students with various challenges. Those labelled *Appreciating drama* ask students to draw diagrams, answer questions, study scripts and generally think about what drama means, how it works and why it is important. They are concerned with the theoretical aspects of the course. They usually require some logbook activity. Stagecraft tasks labelled *Making drama* and *Performing drama* suggest brief and easy exercises and games that can be carried out in the classroom at any time. These are practical exercises which should lead to discussion and a deeper understanding of the subject.

On Your Feet

These are practical drama workshop sessions. It is envisaged that they take place in a 'drama room', rather than a classroom, so students can move and work with comfort and safety. These workshops could run over a number of classes.

The exercises in the *On your feet* sections usually begin with warm-up, relaxation and concentration exercises. These are followed by a selection of group exercises and practical tasks, and usually culminate in a presentation of some form, and recording the session in logbooks.

Unit assessment

A unit could last for four weeks. Or six. Or a full term. If you are studying *Commedia*, for example, then the time spent on the unit will vary from group to group, depending on a range of influences, including the experience of the students. The *Unit assessment* is there to sum up the unit's work in a practical fashion. It usually involves students working in a group towards a fully developed performance. The journey will take time to complete. It must be recorded in the logbooks.

How to use the logbook

The first thing the drama student needs to do is buy a strong, sturdy exercise book. This is the logbook. The logbook is a personal diary that should be taken to all drama classes. It will become a record of the year's work.

The logbook is there for the recording of all practical drama work; anything at all that relates to the business of theatre and performance. It is also a notebook, and as such will serve as a record of the work done and the topics studied in the theoretical section of the course.

Finally, it is a personal diary.

Here are some guidelines.

Practical drama

- After a practical drama session it is a good idea to record any breathing exercises, voice exercises and warm-up routines that work for you. Remember them, so that you will be able to use them for yourself later on.
- Record any exercises and games from the practical sessions that you enjoyed and found useful.
- Record any personal insights that you have gained from your practical drama activities. Record your failures as well as your successes. What have you learnt about yourself?
- Comment on your experiences of working in a group. How are ideas and energy built up within a group? Analyse why a particular activity succeeded or failed. What have you learnt from working with others in a group?
- What have you learnt from your practical sessions about the art of acting?
- Record your own reviews of plays you have seen. What have you learnt about theatre from your own experience of seeing plays as well as your own reading of theatre reviews and newspaper articles?
- Stick clippings from newspapers, magazines and theatre programs into your logbook.
- Add sketches, diagrams and photographs.

Drama theory

- Your work on the theory of drama, or the study of a particular period or style of theatre outlined in *Part two* of this book, should be done in your logbook.
- This should include written pieces, set designs, blocking diagrams, costume sketches, questionnaires, scriptwriting, research work and character charts.

Personal diary

- As this is a personal diary you may add your own observations on any aspect of the course at any time.
- Stick in photographs of people, scenes, props or costumes that interest you, and which might stimulate ideas for playbuilding or character work.
- Add any research work of your own.
- Record any personal stories or fresh angles that you might bring to your studies.
- Include your thoughts, ideas and broodings on the progress of any practical work; whether it be a workshop session, project work, or rehearsals for the public performance of a play.
- Record an analysis of the characters you play, and the various acting techniques and approaches you bring to acting each role.
- Include any words of wisdom that emerge from classroom discussions.

The logbook teaches you to teach yourself. It helps you form your own ideas and draw your own conclusions about a piece of theatre or a particular performance.

You must always be honest when writing in this book. If you do so it will help you assess your own strengths and weaknesses as a researcher, as an observer and as an actor.

Aim to fill three pages a week.

Although the logbook is a personal diary, it is also a book that the teacher will read: so be tactful.

Part One

Playbuilding

Chapter 1

Starting the journey

Outcomes

In this section you will:

- contribute, select, develop, and structure ideas in an improvisation

- explore characters and relationships through improvisation techniques

- collaborate in developing planned and spontaneous improvisations

- record and reflect on your practical work.

Improvisation

Playbuilding is about building by playing.

Drama is the most practical of team sports. It is also about *working with others* to build a piece of theatre or short play.

So where do you start?

With a discussion? Possibly, though this can lead to problems because everyone has different ideas: 'This idea will not work', 'This idea is better than that one', 'This idea has been done before'.

The truth is that everything has been done before. Also, it is impossible to say whether a particular idea will work or not. It is probably true to say that every idea can work – if you are able to find a right way to do it. Good drama is not just a question of hitting on a winning idea. A piece of live theatre will be successful if a group of performers approach it in an original and imaginative fashion. The answer lies not so much in what you do as in how you do it.

'Drama' means 'things done'. It does not mean 'things that could have been done if we had more time' or 'things that might have been done if only the others had followed my ideas'.

The best way for a small group of actors to start building a piece of theatre, then, is to get up and do it. This is called improvisation.

To improvise means to make something up as you go along. In drama, that means play.

As children we knew all about improvisation. We could lose ourselves in a story. We could imagine we were a wizard, believe a stick to be a magic wand and our backyard to be an enchanted forest. We managed to do this without an ounce of self-consciousness and with a great deal of energy.

As we grew older we lost the ability to become spontaneously involved in make-believe.

Before we approach the process of playbuilding, we need to rediscover our imaginative and creative skills by relearning the art of improvisation. We are all capable of becoming nimble improvisers. Here's how to do it.

How to improvise

Actors refer to an improvisation as an 'impro'.

A group of three actors takes the stage for an impro. They may know where they are, for example in a hospital, but they know nothing else. What happens next? One of the performers pretends to be a doctor. He walks around like a doctor and says to one of the female actors, 'How is the patient coming along, nurse?'. At this point the third performer might lie down and pretend to be in great pain. The nurse replies, 'Not too well, Doctor'. The scene develops from there.

This is how children play the game of doctors and nurses.
It's not pre-planned.
They make it up as they go along.

There are some techniques, however, which you as a drama student need to know to enable you to think on your feet. They will help you to improvise in an imaginative and creative way and hopefully lead to an entertaining performance.

Offer

In improvisation, an *offer* is the term used to describe anything that is done to gain a reaction.

In pairs, develop a short dialogue starting with one of these verbal offers:
- 'How is the patient coming along, nurse?'
- 'Does having six fingers present any problems for you?'
- 'Give me the $100 I lent you!'
- 'What did your mum say when she caught you?'
- 'You copied my homework!'

How did the dialogues develop? Discuss the results.

Block

In improvisation, to *block* means to give a negative response to an offer. If you block an offer, then the impro collapses.

In the previous exercise, if anyone responded to the offers with comments like these:
- 'What patient?'
- 'I don't have six fingers.'
- 'I didn't lend you anything.'
- 'What are you on about?'
- 'I did not!'

then they were not improvising. The impro has been blocked. There is nowhere for it to go.

Accept

In improvisation, to *accept* means that you say 'yes' to an offer. This will allow an impro to continue. In other words, accepting means taking on board what has been said and going along with it. A good improviser will not only accept an offer, but will try to extend it.

Extend

In improvisation, to *extend* means to develop and explore the original offer. When questioned about her patient the nurse might reply: 'She looked terrible when she came back from the operation'.

This allows the impro to continue; however, it still leaves the doctor with the responsibility of developing the scene. A good improviser will try to advance the scene by throwing in a few ideas of their own.

Advance

In improvisation, to *advance* means to contribute a new idea to help the impro move forward. Here, the nurse might reply, 'The operation was a success. But when she

woke up, I could hear this rattling sound. You'll never guess what they've done ...'
This gives the group a new direction to explore and some fresh ideas to play with. It adds a further dimension to the improvisation.

Stagecraft

Appreciating drama: How to improvise

By using the basic techniques described above, actors can develop the innate creative skills we all possess.

In your logbook, make an entry explaining: offer, block, accept, extend, and advance *in your own words*.

On Your Feet

Playbuilding: Workshop 1

Warm-up
The warm-up phase of a workshop is a means of getting a group focused, alert and prepared to attack the practical learning tasks.

Charades
Charades is a great actors' game. It forces you to communicate clearly, think under pressure and control your audience without resorting to words. It enables you to become adept at using and reading body language.
- Form two teams.
- Each person writes the title of a film, book, TV program or song on a piece of paper and hands it to the group leader.
- Group leaders swap their pile of suggestions with each other. Each group will act out in charade the other group's suggestions.
- Review the conventional gestures used for charades, e.g. 'how many words?', 'syllables', 'sounds like', 'the whole thing', 'film', 'book', 'yes'. All players must use these conventions.
- The game continues until each person has participated.

Exercises
These exercises will help you develop your impro techniques.

Impro techniques
The first exercise asks you to experiment with non-verbal offers. Gestures, facial expressions, body language and movement can be equally effective in developing improvisations. In pairs, choose from the following list of places, and develop a scene in which you communicate with your partner without using words.
- in a cinema
- at a football match
- outside the principal's office
- in a mosh pit
- on an elephant

In the same pairs and in the same place, make up a verbal offer and develop it by using the impro techniques of accepting, extending and advancing that you have just learnt.

The best examples of both these exercises could be presented to the class.

Once you have mastered these techniques you will be able to improvise your way in any situation.

On Your Feet (continued)

Space-jump
This exercise helps members of a group get to know each other. It also gives good practice relating to, and working with, other actors in changing situations. It develops memory skills.
- Members of a group are numbered 1, 2, 3, 4, and so on. Begin with groups of four.
- The first player, alone on stage, is given a setting (for example: a laundromat). The player starts to improvise a scene in that setting, using mime or dialogue or both. After a minute, the command 'Space-jump' freezes the actor in position.
- The second player enters, notes the exact position of player number 1 (the shape of the body, the angle of the head, the position of the arms, and so on.) and begins to act out a fresh scene inspired by that frozen shape. The first player comes to life and instinctively joins in the new scene without any preliminary discussion. The cues are verbal and visual.
- This second scene lasts a minute before the command 'Space-jump' is repeated. The two actors freeze, and the third member of the group initiates the next scene inspired by the exact positions of the two frozen forms. It's an imaginative leap, a space-jump.
- The process is repeated.
- By the time the whole team of four players is on stage, the command 'Space-jump' induces the usual freeze, but signals the exit of the most recent player, number 4. The remaining three actors now revert to the previous scene they played together, but must cleverly move into it starting with their immediate frozen shapes. Stronger players will be able to continue the scene from where they left it.
- The next space-jump is the cue for player number 3 to leave. Those remaining revert to the previous scene they played together, and so on.
- The process ends with the first player on-stage in the laundromat.

Play a number of space-jump games, alternating the order of the members of your group in the process. Some given situations might be:
- on a TV cooking program
- visiting a psychiatrist
- in a changing room cubicle at David Jones
- in a telephone box
- underwater
- on the film set of a Western
- on a building site
- at the hairdressers
- under a bed.

Advanced task
Once you have mastered space-jump in groups of four, see if the whole class can complete a round.

Show me ...
Show me develops your ability to accept and extend offers.

All students stand in the space by themselves. As each offer is made, make the shape with your body. Don't look at what others are doing. Allow your own interpretation to come through.

Make these shapes with your bodies.

Numbers
- Using you whole body, show me the number 1. Allow ten seconds, then repeat with: 2, 7, 9, 3, 8, 10, 5, 6 and 4.

Letters
- Using your whole body, show me the letter A. Then, C, K, P, O, S, X, Z, B, W, V and Z.

Objects
Now find a partner. Stand opposite them and without speaking, together create the following objects. (Don't tell your partner what to do. As an idea forms, add to it. Build it together.)
- a knife and fork (20 seconds)
- a pair of chop sticks (Don't worry about what others are doing.)
- a cup and saucer
- egg on toast

Now find another pair, and form groups of four. Together create the following objects. (Try to follow the group's idea. Don't impose your own; yield to the group.)
- a vase of flowers

On Your Feet (continued)

- a cappuccino
- a flat white
- a garbage bin

Now form groups of eight. Together create the following objects. (With more people, it's much harder. Still try to follow the group's idea.)

- a piano
- a helicopter
- a hamburger
- a microwave
- a watermelon

How difficult did you find it to yield to the group idea? Yielding to the group is not easy. It takes practice.

Advanced task

Form one large group. Together create the following objects.

- a bus
- the same bus with its lights on in the rain
- a computer and keyboard
- a fence
- the Sydney Harbour Bridge

Supermarket mime

The supermarket mime also requires you to accept offers, to extend and advance but over a sustained period.

- The group stands at the side of the working space. Think back to the last time you were in a supermarket. What sorts of people did you see there? Shoppers, checkout operators, shelf-stackers, managers, salespersons, special promotions people. Choose a role or character to take into the space.
- One person begins by walking into the space and acting as if they are in a supermarket.
- The rest of the group observe for a short time, and then enter, one at a time. Once the geography is established, for example where the checkouts are, how the aisles go, where the freezers are, and so on, the actors must observe what has been established. Do not walk into a display of toilet rolls!
- Once six people are moving in the space, someone commands 'Freeze'. The actors stop and must answer all questions put to them. Specific details are required. What kind of trolley do you have? What actual items are in the trolley? Where are the bar codes on the items being scanned? How much is it? Where is the checkout? Who is operating it? And so on.
- The exercise starts again with another six students.
- It continues until everyone has participated.
- Now the supermarket is an all-night supermarket, and it's 3am. The actors must demonstrate character, attitudes, different tempo rhythms, and so on. (Some people may be in a hurry, some may be half-asleep.) What are the attitudes of the people working there? Do they like the night shift? Characters must interact with each other.
- It continues until everyone has participated.

Advanced task

Apply the same process to different public spaces: a library, a sporting event, a cafeteria, an airport, and a building site. Increase the players from six to twelve. Or more.

Stagecraft

Appreciating drama: Workshop summary

Here is a summary of what was learned in the workshop. Make a record in your logbook.
- The warm-up phase in a workshop is a means of getting a group focused, alert and prepared to attack the practical learning tasks.
- *Space-jump* helps members of a group get to know each other. It also gives good practice relating to, and working with, other actors in changing situations.
- Body language often will tell us more about how someone is feeling than what they say.
- *Show me ...* develops your ability to yield to and add to offers.
- *Supermarket mime* gives you practice in yielding to offers, extending and advancing over a sustained period.

Now describe the workshop from your own point of view.
- Which students were the best at charades? Why?
- Did you find it helped to have a number of people collaborating in the improvisation?
- Did thinking in specific detail about what you were doing help to give you physical things to do and relate to?

The elements of drama

The drama syllabus defines the 'elements of drama'. This refers to the common language we should use when discussing and analysing our work.

Character	The representing of a three-dimensional human being with a particular personality, characteristics and background
Role	The representing of a point of view, and identifying with a set of values and attitudes
Status	A character's position and standing, weighty or otherwise, within any grouping of people
Conflict	Characters are in conflict when they have opposing purposes or objectives within the drama
Dramatic tension	The problems faced by a character: their relationships, the creation of surprise, the unfolding of mystery
Focus	The performer's focus in creating concentration and belief The audience's focus on the dramatic situation
Place	The setting of the dramatic action
Time	The period in which the dramatic action takes place
Situation	The circumstances the characters are in
Space	The stage area, the spatial design of the set and the arrangement of the physical elements of performance
Language	The verbal and non-verbal forms in which the dramatic action is conveyed

Navigating Drama

CHARACTER → ROLE ↓ STATUS ↓ CONFLICT ↓ DRAMATIC TENSION ↓ FOCUS ↓ PLACE ↓ TIME ↓ SITUATION ↓ SPACE ← LANGUAGE ← MOVEMENT ← SOUND ← RHYTHM ↑ STRUCTURE ↑ SYMBOLS ↑ ATMOSPHERE ↑ DRAMATIC MEANING ↑ AUDIENCE ENGAGEMENT

Moment	The control and manipulation of key moments in the dramatic action.
Sound	The aural devices to enhance performance.
Rhythm	The manipulation of timing through pace and tempo.
Structure	The framework through which the content of the drama is presented.
Symbols	The visual imagery of language, movement, gesture, objects and staging used to reinforce meaning.
Atmosphere	The feeling or mood created by, and emerging through, the dramatic action.
Dramatic meaning	The sum total of what is communicated between the performers and the audience.
Audience engagement	The ultimate purpose of all the elements of drama.

Stagecraft

Appreciating drama: The elements of drama

To help you become familiar with these terms, complete one of the following in your logbook.
- Create your own full-page diagram that represents all the elements of drama in one illustration.
  Or
- Copy out all the words from the list above, but illustrate each of them with a picture instead of a definition.

Spontaneous improvisation

When improvisation is spontaneous it means that it is unprepared.

As we have seen, actors act out a situation responding to each other on the spot without any prior planning. This is an exciting way to work as no one knows where it will lead.

Navigating Drama

Stagecraft

Making drama: Impro with given place and time

Some people find it easy to respond spontaneously. Others find it more difficult. The following exercise will encourage you to react spontaneously and get your creative and imaginative juices flowing.

Form groups of four. Each group may improvise any scene they like, but must do so in a given place and/or time.

Here are some ideas to get you started. In this impro you may choose any one topic, or mix and match two topics, one from the 'place' column and one from the 'time' column.

Place	Time
In a retirement home	In the year AD 2096
In a police station	After dark
In a foreign restaurant	During the second world war
In jail	In the heat of the day
In an underground car park	In the dark ages
On a distant planet	In the early days of the colony
In a law court	During a thunderstorm
In an outback shack	An hour before the big event
On a skyscraper	Ten minutes after the big event

- Don't forget that it is important to respond positively to the drama.
- Do not try to steal the scene or upstage the others in the group.
- Do not argue when someone introduces a new direction or fresh idea. Always accept what you have been given, use your impro technique and try to extend and advance the idea. Run with it, develop it, and see where it will take you.
- If you do not like the general direction in which things are going, don't worry – forget about any final result. Relax. Let go. Follow your creative instincts.

Stagecraft

Making drama: Impro from pictures and photographs

Pictures, photographs and drawings can provide inspiration for a spontaneous improvisation. It is a good idea to bring pictures and photographs of your own into class.

- Work in groups of four. Each group is given a picture or photograph that they haven't seen before, and must use it as inspiration for a spontaneous improvisation.
- Alternatively, look at these three cartoons by Leunig (on pages 13–14). Still working in groups of four, select one of them. Study it for no more than 20 seconds. Then get up, improvise your scene and see where it leads you.

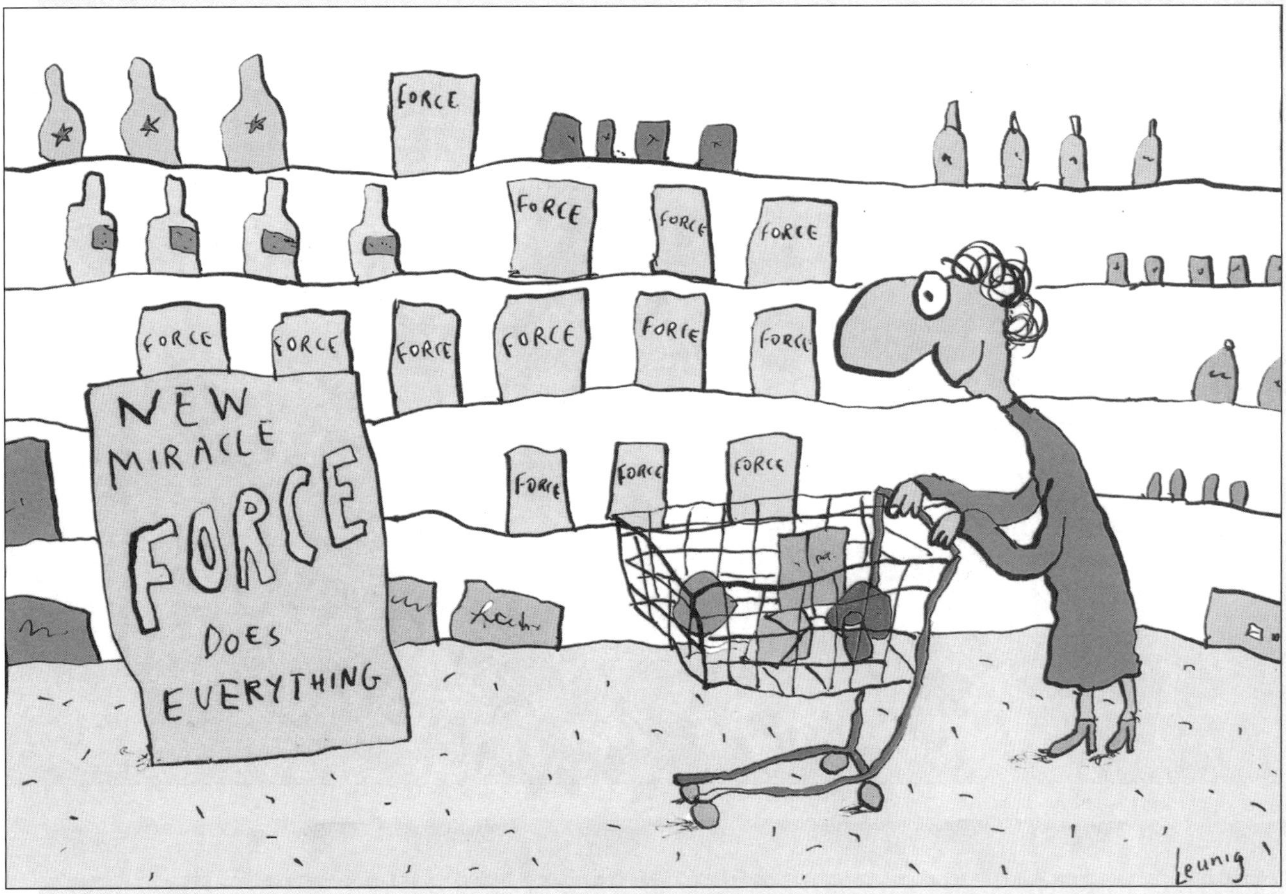
NEW MIRACLE FORCE DOES EVERYTHING
FORCE
Leunig

"We're all lying in the gutter but some of us are looking at the stars"
NICOLE
RUSSELL
KYLIE

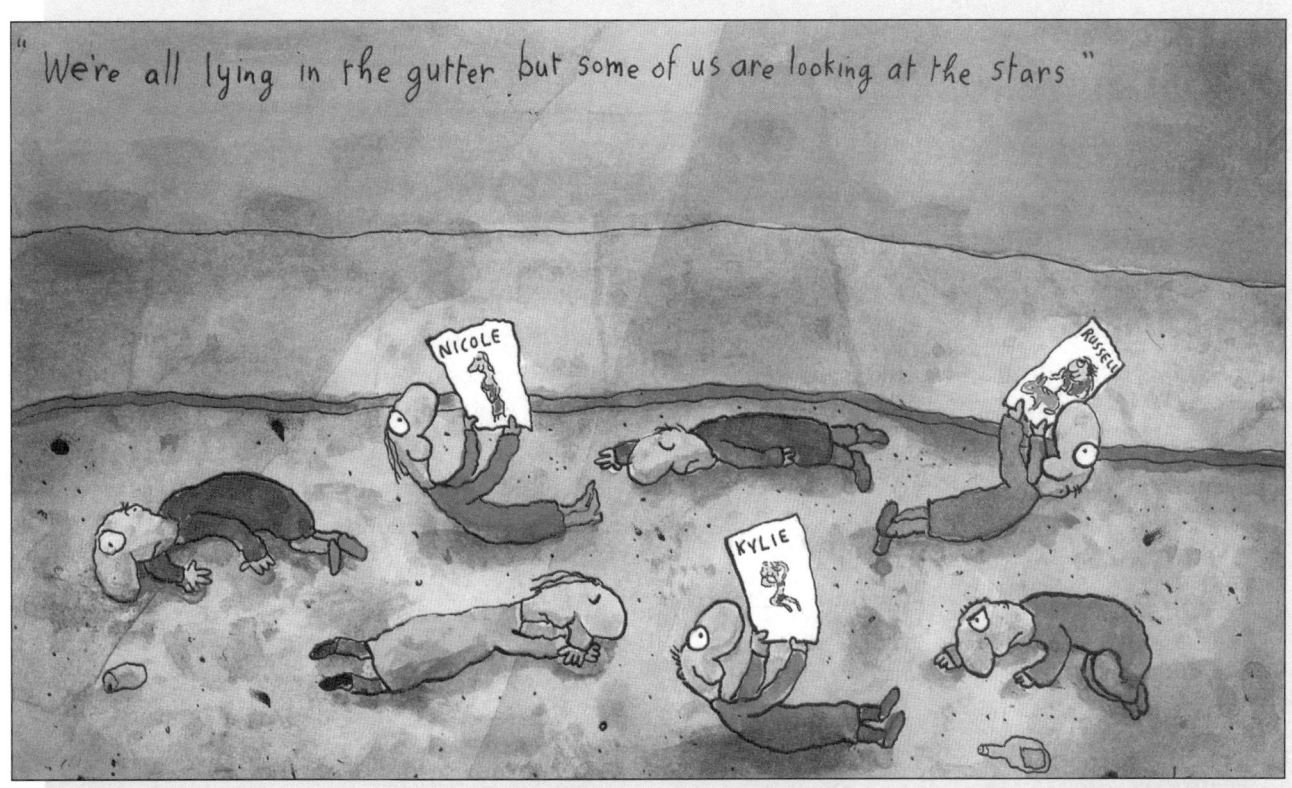

On Your Feet

Playbuilding: Workshop 2

Warm-up

Spontaneous improvisation requires you to become adept at quick thinking. Warm-up exercises help you focus on the moment.

Alphabet mime

Alphabet mime can be played sitting or standing in a circle. Each player must mime as many objects as they can beginning with the letter of the alphabet they are given.
- Time limit: 30 seconds.
- Those watching call out the objects mimed.
- Players must touch their nose when the mime is guessed correctly, or they forfeit the point.
- Judges time the mime and count the correct guesses.
- Players lose a point if they make any sound whatsoever.
- This continues until everyone has participated.

Opposites

Opposites is about lying. It trains you to respond quickly under pressure.

Each person takes a turn sitting in front of the group and must answer all questions without hesitating, laughing or telling the truth. Before starting, make sure everyone has chosen a question to ask. Simple questions are best, for example: 'Are you wearing socks?', 'Are your eyes blue?'. Only questions requiring a yes/no answer can be asked. Ask them at speed. If you laugh, hesitate or accidentally tell the truth, you're out. The person who asked the question then takes over.

Exercises

These exercises help you to work in small groups and develop your spontaneous impro techniques.

TV guide

Cut out several synopses of films and soapy episodes from newspapers or TV guides, put them

On Your Feet (continued)

in a hat and pick one out. The group, consisting of four players, must then act out the given scene. In an exercise like this just leap in and see what happens. No prior discussion is allowed.

The best way to get started is with one actor assuming a role and a second joining in. The others then become part of the act when they sense an opening.

Here are some suggestions.
- Julie is looking forward to a visit from her old school friend Peggy; however, things aren't quite as Julie expects.
- An actress sues a film company when her life is ruined by cosmetic surgery.
- Rosemary and Terence's intimate evening is ruined when the police arrive at their front door.
- Jim and Roy become involved in a dangerous situation in outer space.
- A group of friends falls out during a weekend in the country.
- Two young lovers find themselves caught in a web of corruption in Naples.
- Sally has been asked to act in a television advertisement promoting a product she despises.
- Chuck and Michelle are curious about the new neighbours, so Jenny invites them over for dinner.
- Brian returns from a fishing trip to find that Claudia has some terrible news.

Impro with given characters

In this approach, members of the group may improvise any scene they like, but must do so in a given character. A good way to create a distinctive character is to go back to the medieval idea of the four humours. At that time it was believed that a person's character was made up of a mixture of the four substances: bile (malencolye), phlegm, choler, and blood (sangwyn). Although it was thought important to balance these substances, it was realised that some people possessed more of one substance than of the others.

- The melancholic character (earth) is cold, dry, heavy, moody, depressed, analytical, thoughtful, artistic, sensitive, philosophical and idealistic.
- The phlegmatic character (water) is easy-going, relaxed, patient, well-balanced, quiet, witty, fearful, unenthusiastic, shy and self-righteous.
- The choleric character (fire) was bossy, impatient, inflexible, unsympathetic, dynamic, active, unemotional, independent, confident and a born leader.
- The sanguine character (air) was talkative, amusing, emotional, cheerful, curious, sincere, egotistical, naive, childish, angry and controlled by circumstances.

Work in groups of four. In this improvisation, each performer must adopt one of these character types. Take a minute to look over the character traits, and then once again launch into an improvisation and see what happens.

Inspiration from newspaper headlines

Take a daily newspaper into the workshop. It will most likely be full of comic, dramatic and unexpected stories. Use one of them as inspiration for a group scene. Here are some examples for you to work from.

The Feathers are Flying at Swansdowne
Mrs Swansdowne is accused of lowering the tone of the street by deliberately hanging out her washing in a provocative way.

I'll Love My Man Forever
Sydney wife proclaims her husband's innocence and lashes out at photographers while visiting her terrorist husband in a Paris jail.

Done Like A Doughnut
Armed bandits wear a glazed look as they break into the Krispy Kreme doughnut shop while attempting to put a hole in the shop's profits.

Japanese Businessman Hires Actor to Perform His Home Duties For Him
Busy Yashuri Meguro finds that his work consumes so much of his time that he is unable to perform effectively at home.

Suburban Housewife Becomes Property Millionaire
'My life has changed dramatically', she says, 'Even the simplest things have become complicated'.

Lawyer Vanishes Without A Trace
Mr Brendan Vincenti, due to take part in the notorious Fielden case, checks his baggage in at Sydney airport and then disappears.

Navigating Drama

Stagecraft

Appreciating drama: Workshop summary

Spontaneous improvisation requires you to become adept at thinking quickly and responding under pressure. Answer these questions in your logbook.
- How did you cope with pressure in *Opposites*?
- *TV guide* gave you no opportunity to plan. How did you respond?
- *Impro with given characters* made you improvise the where, when and why. How did your group cope with this challenge?
- What have you discovered about how you react under pressure?
- Take a few minutes to write an honest self-assessment of how you are progressing in mastering the art of improvisation.

Role

Role: Representing a point of view, identifying with values and attitudes of others.

In life we play many roles.

You may be a son or daughter, a student, a friend, an expert and a sportsperson all at the same time. At different times and with different people we all play different roles.

Understanding views, values and attitudes other than your own can add depth and complexity to your work in drama. Sometimes you will need to portray characters and roles that are very different from your own.

Chapter 1 Starting the journey

Stagecraft
Making drama: Whole group role-play

Improvisation skills are used in this exercise that asks the whole group to participate spontaneously.
- Everyone sits in a large circle.
- One actor takes on the role of a detective who will question the others about a make-believe incident.
- The detective enters the circle, introduces themselves and explains that this is an investigation into a bank robbery that occurred yesterday afternoon.
- Everyone is asked 'Who are you?', and they make up a character in the story and then role-play that character in answer to all further questions.
- The detective asks leading questions around the circle so that a story is built up through the responses.
- Early questions to different players might be 'How long have you been working at the bank?', 'What were you doing in the bank?', 'What did you do after you held up the teller?', and 'What happened after you were asked to lie down on the floor?'.
- New players must relate to the characters, situation, space and dramatic tension that has already been *determined* by previous questioning.
- A story develops.
- The role-play continues as long as the story continues to hold together.

Dramatic Tension: Problems faced by a character, creation of surprise, unfolding of mystery.

Although large group role-plays can become complicated, there are nevertheless advantages in having other people support and assist you in creating an improvisation. Working off and using what other performers give you is fundamental to producing successful drama.

Stagecraft
Making drama: Jack

Jack is a Year Nine student.

He has been suspended for graffitiing the science building. He has been in trouble several times before. A meeting has been called to decide if he is to return to school. Attending the meeting are Jack; Judy and Alex (Jack's Mum and Dad); Lucy (a fellow student who wants to speak in Jack's defence); Dr Simms (the principal); and Mrs McFadden (the teacher responsible for student welfare). At the conclusion of the meeting the principal will advise Jack of his decision.
- In groups of six, cast the roles and improvise the meeting.
- End the role-play with the principal giving his decision and explaining the reasons for it.
- Change roles and re-enact the scenario.
- Discuss your observations.

Navigating Drama

Stagecraft

Making drama: Welfare agency

- Work in groups of six.
- Three students are to be the committee members of the welfare agency.
- Three students are to be applicants needing financial assistance.
- The welfare committee operates under these conditions:
  - you have $600 available this week
  - there are three applicants
  - you must decide who will receive the money.

Applicant 1: Judy Doyle. 26 years old. You are a single mother in desperate straits who needs the money to take your child to Melbourne where your family can take care of you.

Applicant 2: Robert Brown. 19 years old. You have been unemployed for over a year. You have a job interview tomorrow and need money to buy some decent clothes.

Applicant 3: John Fitzpatrick. 46 years old. You have a part-time job but it doesn't pay well. You can't afford to pay the rent or eat proper food. There is no heating in your flat. You need money because your health is suffering.

- The committee calls in each applicant and interviews them.
- The applicants leave the room after their interview.
- After the interviews the committee has five minutes to come to a decision.
- We listen to their discussion.
- The applicants are called back into the room and are informed of the decision.
- The chairperson explains the reasons for the decision.

Status

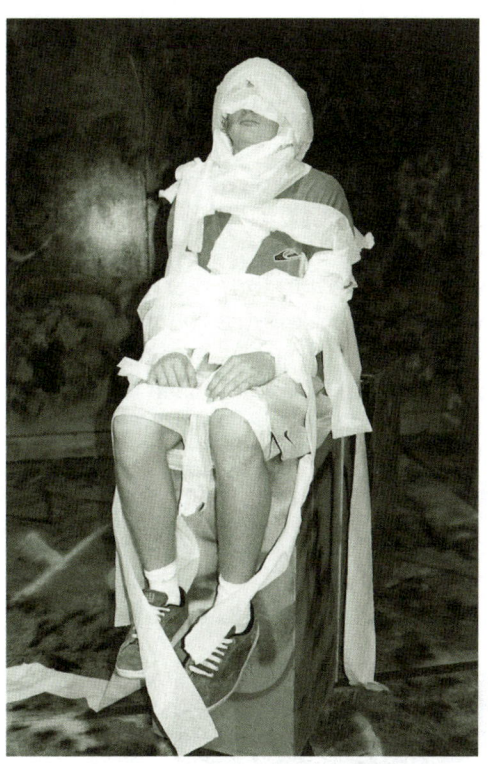

Linked with the different roles we play is the idea of *status*.

Status is concerned with our position in society. Which roles in the following pairs do you think have the higher status?

Principal	Student
Child	Parent
Team member	Coach
Conductor	Musician
Citizen	Mayor

Improvised scenes often reflect the different status of characters. The status of a character may change according to the role and the situation.

Status is often reflected physically, through body language.

Status: A character's position. Their social standing within a group of people.

Stagecraft

Making drama: Exploring status

Activity 1
In pairs, chose one combination from the list above. Make an entrance into the space and stand as if you are posing for a photograph.

When this is completed, discuss the differences and similarities in the body language of the high- and low-status characters.

Activity 2
With the same partner as before, act out a pair of the following combinations.

Stand straight and still	Stoop and fidget
Feet angled to the side	Feet apart and pointed ahead
Arms covering stomach	Arms by their sides
Head held to the side	Head held high
Moving in straight lines	Wandering about
Averting eyes	Maintaining eye contact
Speaking clearly	Mumbling

Which member of each pair is exhibiting the high-status behaviour? How do you know? Discuss your findings.

Navigating Drama

Stagecraft

Appreciating drama: Recording status

- Copy the list of combinations from the previous Stagecraft exercise into your logbook.
- Record your findings about each of them.
- Add any examples of high and low status that you observed while watching the actors perform. For example, what did you notice about their rhythms, focus and personal space?

Adopting high-status physical characteristics can help you to feel and think like a high-status person. Similarly, adopting low-status characteristics can make you feel lower in the pecking order.

This is a technique you can use to your advantage in life. If you have to give a speech for example, and you are feeling nervous, consciously try to adopt high-status characteristics. Plant your feet, hold up your head and look your audience in the eye. You will appear to be confident and therefore start to feel so.

Always use the concept of status in an improvisation and you will have more options both physically and verbally.

Stagecraft

Making drama: Reversing the status

In pairs choose one of these status pairings and improvise a short scene, but reverse the status. For example, give the principal low-status characteristics and attitudes, and make the student high status.

Take five minutes to develop the impro and then present the results.

Principal	Student
Child	Parent
Team member	Coach
Conductor	Musician
Citizen	Mayor

Usually when you alter the expected status, the result will be comic.

Conflict

> **Conflict:** Characters with opposing purposes and objectives within the drama.

Drama thrives on conflict.

Everyone has their own point of view. People have different values. No two people are the same. Sooner or later this will lead to conflict. If characters are in conflict then we are interested to watch them. We want to see what will happen, who will win or who is proved right.

In drama, conflict is not so much about fights and arguments, but more about opposing purposes and objectives.

Stagecraft
Making drama: Exploring conflict

Without any preparation, two performers act out the following scenes in front of the group.
- Two friends are having a drink in a bar. They talk about the weather, the news and their families. They agree with each other about everything.
- Two friends are having a drink in a bar. They talk about the weather, the news and their families. They disagree with each other about everything.
- Two friends are having a drink in a bar. One of them wants another drink, while the other tries to get the friend to leave. No touching is allowed.
- Two friends are having a drink in a bar. One of them has just been left by their partner and is very upset, full of self-blame. The other one tries to comfort them. You may repeat this exercise a few times. The results may be different.
Discuss your observations. Which scenes worked best, and why?
Make your own notes in your logbook. Discuss all four scenes. What have you learnt about conflict?

Navigating Drama

Stagecraft
Making drama: Power-play improvisations

Two actors take the stage. They are each privately handed a piece of paper. On each is written an objective. Neither sees the other's objective. Without any preparation they must improvise a scene, each trying to fulfil their own objective. Set a time limit of four minutes. There will be a winner and a loser. Here are some suggestions.

- A young man is on his first date. *The young man* is *determined* that the evening will be a success. *The girl* does not want to upset him, but she is feeling ill and wants to go home.
- A young woman is applying for a loan. She has just got married and wants a loan so that she can buy her first house. *The bank manager* is happy to lend money to old and trusted customers but does not trust younger applicants.
- A young couple has just bought their first house. *He* is proud that they have finally got a place of their own that they can have to themselves. *She* wants her sick, elderly mother to come and stay with them.

Conflict is central to drama. You will have noted that conflict works best when it is not presented in too obvious a way. In the power-play impros the best results were probably those where the actors did not make their objectives known too soon.

You might also have realised that a character can be in conflict with themselves. This was true of the person in the bar in the Stagecraft exercise on page 21, who had been deserted by a partner.

When playbuilding, always remember the importance of conflict.

Planned improvisation

Situation: The circumstances the characters are in.

In a planned improvisation the actors discuss the impro beforehand.

They may discuss who the characters are, where they are, what they are doing and what happens. Or they might only decide on some of these things. Nevertheless, they will not plan the impro moment by moment. If all the details are planned, then it is not an improvisation but a re-enactment.

Improvisation is a creative process. Often you do not know where it will lead or what will be discovered. This next exercise takes you through some approaches to a planned impro.

Stagecraft
Making drama: Impro from songs and poetry

Songs and poems can provide inspiration for a prepared improvisation. It is a good idea to bring some songs, verses and poems into class and, in groups, discuss which ones you would like to explore using prepared improvisation.

Give yourself about five minutes preparation time. Then see what happens.

Chapter 1 Starting the journey

On Your Feet

Playbuilding: Workshop 3

Warm-up

These warm-up exercises help students to relax and focus their concentration on the tasks at hand.

What are you doing?

- Form a circle.
- Player 1 steps into the circle and mimes an assigned action – say, conducting an orchestra.
- As Player 1 begins conducting an orchestra, the next person in line asks 'What are you doing?'. Player 1 responds with the first thing that comes to mind, for example: 'Skinning a cat'. They never say what they are actually doing.
- Player 2 steps in and starts to mime skinning a cat. The next person in line asks, 'What are you doing?'. This game continues around the circle.
- Try to use the whole space for your mime. Go for speed and pace.

Remote control

One person acts as the remote control. The rest of the class divides into groups of three or four. Each group represents a TV channel. Choose a channel from this list or make up you own.

Channel 1	The News at six
Channel 2	The Shopping Channel
Channel 3	The Simpsons
Channel 4	A soap
Channel 5	Jerry Springer
Channel 6	Lawn bowls, live
Channel 7	The Weather Channel
Channel 8	Movie of the week

Everyone freezes. The remote control clicks towards the channels one at a time. The TV shows come to life when the remote control announces their channel. They freeze when the remote control clicks to another channel. Change the channels at random.

On Your Feet (continued)

Exercises

These exercises help you to work in small groups and develop your planned impro techniques.

Breakfast mime

Using your bodies to create props and objects in improvisations provides an element of interest and can result in creative solutions to problems.

Work in groups of five to six.
- Each group chooses one person to act out all the things done between waking up in the morning and leaving for school.
- All the objects used or handled in this process are to be made by the bodies of the rest of the group. They will need to be chairs, spoons, the shower, anything and everything that is used.
- Allow ten minutes for planning and developing.
- Present your impro to the class.

'I'll have the usual'

Students learning how to improvise often say they find the most difficult part is knowing what to say. You can overcome this by doing three things:
- apply your impro technique (offer, accept, extend and advance)
- listen
- observe.

This exercise will give you practice in doing these three things.
- In small groups spend five minutes planning a restaurant scene.
- One person should play a waiter and the others be customers.
- Plan who you are, why you are out to dinner, the time and what will happen.
- Don't plan the dialogue.
- Set up the restaurant tables and present the scenes.

How did each group respond? Could you observe performers listening and observing? How did you respond? Did you have any problems with knowing what to do or say?

Now, in the same restaurants, form different groups, choose one of the following scenarios and go through the same process.
- A family argues over the bill.
- A group of vegetarians finds themselves in a steakhouse.
- A waiter arrives who doesn't speak English.
- There is a fly in your mother's soup.
- You are on a blind date that goes horribly wrong.

Inspiration from mime and movement

This exercise asks you to develop a dramatic improvisation through movement alone.

Form groups of four or five.

The entrance. In your group, enter a room. Who enters first? What sort of time gap exists between the entrances of each member of the group? At what speed does each person enter the room? Explore slow motion. Once the actors have come through the door they take up positions in the room. Create a sense of drama by movement and facial expression. What has been happening before the entrance? Maybe one person is clearly upset, while another is staring hard at a third. Expectations are being built up, moods are being explored.

The action. It doesn't matter what each of the actors does next, but each must do something. If a piece of material is lying on the floor of the room, one actor could wrap it around themselves, all the time nervously glancing around at the others, who glare menacingly back. If there is a window in the corner, someone could go and stare silently out of it. If a book is on the desk, a third actor could sit and rip the pages out in slow motion while the others react in horror. If there is a piano in the room, an actor could walk slowly over to it and then, while all were staring apprehensively, play a single bass note. Dramatic tension is being established.

On Your Feet (continued)

The movement. Now move freely around the room. Adjust your clothing as you go. When asked to do so, freeze.
- Freeze in a greeting. Remember your position.
- Freeze as a model in a shop window. Remember your position.
- Freeze in the position of a police officer, teacher, priest, or any other recognisable member of society. Remember your position.
- Grab onto someone else and freeze. Remember your position.
- Grab onto the whole group and freeze. Remember your position.

Stop and discuss what could be happening in these frozen pictures. Shreds of stories are now emerging.

The drama. Now sit down in your group and work out how to add together the elements you have created to make a short, dramatic piece of theatre.

You will need to discuss this carefully beforehand. Where possible, choose the moments that worked best during your workshop sessions, and find ways of connecting them into one performance.

You may use these elements in any order you wish.
- A group entrance.
- Individual actions by two members of the group (with consequent reactions).
- Two individual freeze-frames; either frozen or walked through.
- One group freeze-frame; either frozen or walked through.
- To these you may now add:
  - an exit
  - five different sounds (the sounds may be used more than once)
  - one line of dialogue.

Stagecraft

Appreciating drama: Workshop summary

In your logbooks make a summary of what you did in the workshop by answering the following questions.
- How effective were *What are you doing?* and *Remote control* as warm-up exercises?
- Did *I'll have the usual* help you to respond with dialogue more easily?
- Did *Breakfast mime* and the final movement exercise give you any new insights into the business of playbuilding? What did you discover?

Now discuss the workshop from your point of view.
- Are you more comfortable with non-verbal or verbal impros?
- How successful do you think your group was in the final movement exercise?
- Which was the most successful performance in the final movement exercise? Discuss the reasons for its success.

Unit assessment

Making and performing drama: A planned improvisation

(Four to six lessons' preparation.)

Conditions

In groups of three or four, use the following newspaper article as the stimulus for a planned improvisation.

- You may use any aspect of the article you wish: the situation, the characters, the incidents or the language. You may also approach the improvisation in a non-naturalistic fashion.
- Use any dramatic forms and theatrical devices you feel appropriate, such as:
  - character
  - chorus work
  - conflict
  - dramatic tension
  - focus
  - freeze-frame
  - movement
  - mime
  - narration
  - repetition.
- The improvisation should go for five minutes.
- Rehearsal blacks should be worn.
- Each student should be featured equally in the improvisation.

In your logbook

- Keep a lesson-by-lesson account of your process, for example initial ideas, research, development, visual stimulus, recording of practical sessions, and rehearsals.
- Date all entries.
- After the performance, evaluate your work. What were the strengths and weaknesses of your planned improvisation?

Assessment criteria

- Making, accepting and extending offers in improvisation
- Collaborating with others
- Using a range of vocal and movement skills
- Ability to record the process of rehearsal and performance

Aisle angst: big trouble in trolley land

By JOHN HUXLEY

It was soon after making a lunge for some lychees in her local supermarket that Marion Dove became a victim of trolley rage.

'I suddenly felt this sharp jab in the back of the ankles', she said. 'It was so painful I fell to the ground.

'When I got up and turned around, of course I expected someone to say sorry. There was this man staring at me with hard, cold eyes. 'An apology wouldn't go amiss', I said to him.

Instead, the man – whom Miss Dove describes as a smartly dressed, straight-looking yuppie-type, 'possibly an accountant or a lawyer or something', in his mid to late-30s – accused her of rudeness moments earlier.

'He said I'd pushed his trolley out of the way. Then he just marched off', explained Ms Dove, who works in the costume department at Opera Australia. 'I was completely taken aback. Quite dazed. It sounds so stupid. So trivial. But I was almost in tears.

'I did go round the front of him to reach the lychees but I honestly don't think I touched his trolley. But I mean, whatever I'd done, the idea of someone ramming me quite deliberately ... well, it's just like road rage. A complete over-reaction. And potentially quite dangerous.'

Ms Dove did not feel able to report the incident, which

"Just like road rage"...Woolworths Neutral Bay.

occurred at the Woolworths store at Neutral Bay, to the manager. 'It would have been like running to the teacher in the playground.'

But she told her boyfriend, who joined her soon afterwards. He went in search of her attacker, but could not find him. 'Perhaps it was just as well he didn't.'

Supermarket chiefs yesterday conceded that confrontations between shoppers – more often about queue-jumping – were increasing, but 'trolley rage' was rare.

'I see examples of rage on the roads almost every day, but in the supermarket? Well, I guess it happens, but not often', said Reg Clairs, chief executive officer of Woolworths.

He recalled that one shopper had complained that the Neutral Bay store – perhaps because of its busy, impatient North Shore clientele – was notorious for 'ankle-clippers', though the vast majority of offences were unintentional.

Indeed, Mr Clairs pointed out, Neutral Bay had 'entered popular mythology' as one of Woolies' most friendly stores. Special singles' shopping nights and the adoption of an unofficial code of signals, involving the precise placement of bananas in their trolleys, enabled shoppers to strike up relationships with members of the opposite or same sex.

So successful were the Neutral Bay singles' nights that they were repeated, with shop staff dressed as cupid, when a new store was opened in a Brisbane suburb recently, Mr Clairs said.

Last year in Britain, a shopper was jailed for 28 days for ramming his trolley full of groceries into a customer who had accused him of queue-jumping. Though police have intervened, most recently in Lakemba, in disputes between shoppers, Australia has yet to experience such serious cases.

But experts, such as Leslie Bullock, who runs the Manly Stress Control Centre, warn that the supermarket aisle, like the road, is becoming a leading flashpoint for the pressures of modern living.

'Whatever their problems – screaming kids, financial worries, job insecurity – more people are getting angry and resentful, especially in places such as supermarkets, which can be frustrating.'

An alarming number of people are now living on the edge, Dr Peter Birrell, a senior lecturer in psychology at the University of NSW, said recently.

'You only have to look at the facial expressions of the majority of people in supermarkets in the early evening to see how stressed and sour they look. People are walking around with homicidal thoughts directed at that funny little couple with their trolley parked at an unreasonable angle.'

Or, as Ms Dove painfully discovered, that woman innocently reaching for some lychees.

(Sydney Morning Herald 15/1/98)

Assessment feedback sheet
A planned improvisation

	Level of Achievement		
	Developing	Substantial	Excellent

Performance

Making, accepting and extending offers	1	2	3	4	5
Collaborating with others	1	2	3	4	5
Voice (vocal range and volume)	1	2	3	4	5
Movement (use of body to convey character/role)	1	2	3	4	5

Logbook

Completes entries for each session	1	2	3	4	5
Description of final improvisation	1	2	3	4	5

Teacher's comments

_____
_____
_____
_____
_____
_____
_____

Student's comments on their strengths, as well as areas that need more work, thought and attention

_____
_____
_____
_____
_____
_____
_____
_____

Chapter 2

Navigating playbuilding

Outcomes

In this section you will:

- use improvisation and acting techniques to communicate dramatic meaning

- contribute, select, develop and structure ideas while building an original performance

- develop linear and non-linear scene structures to communicate ideas

- record, reflect and evaluate the process of playbuilding.

Playbuilding

Dramatic Meaning: What is communicated between the actors and the audience.

Playbuilding is about creating an original performance.

Chapter 1 showed you improvisation techniques that you can use to develop your ideas. Chapter 2 will guide you through the process of turning those ideas into a structured dramatic statement.

When there are so many possibilities, the way forward can be daunting; however, there are a range of forms, structures and approaches that will assist you in navigating your way through the maze. You may choose one particular dramatic form, such as mime, clowning, *Commedia dell'Arte* or creative movement; or you may decide to combine elements from a number of different forms and structures.

There is no all-purpose formula for playbuilding. It's more a matter of making decisions about which is the best way to develop and present your ideas to your audience.

Have something to say

You must have something to say. This is the most important requirement in playbuilding. No dramatic structure will be effective unless you have a clear understanding of what you want to convey to your audience.

Throughout history, drama has been used as a tool for drawing attention to events and issues in society.

Around 400BC, Aristophanes wrote an anti-war play called *Lysistrata*. In the play, Lysistrata begins a protest movement designed to stop men making war. She gathers the women of Athens together and persuades them to go on strike. The women refuse to cook, clean, obey or comfort their husbands until they renounce war. The play was humorous and entertaining but had a clear message for its audience about war and its consequences.

Medieval drama also conveyed clear messages. Stories from the Bible and morality plays were acted out to show people how they should live their lives.

In Elizabethan times Shakespeare explored a range of public and private issues. His plays made his audiences think about politics, power, love, honour and family relationships.

Melodrama presented clear messages for the audience. The struggle between vice and virtue always ended with the hero and heroine triumphing over villainy.

Today most television drama conveys messages to the audience. The detective genre for example, is based on variations of the same message: crime does not pay.

Comedy programs such as 'The Simpsons' use humour to highlight the foibles and absurdities of modern life.

We are used to this dramatic convention.

Stagecraft

Appreciating drama: Test the theory

In pairs, make a list in your logbook of the last five television programs you have each watched. Discuss each program and try to determine the message conveyed to the audience. Compare your findings with others.

All drama conveys a message to the audience.

The message may be direct.

It may be subtle.

It may be disguised in humour.

It may be symbolic or abstract, but scratch the surface and you will find it. You can present a strong message with serious dramatic meaning in your piece and still make it theatrically entertaining. Your message, or 'dramatic meaning', is revealed through the action.

Stagecraft

Making drama: Messaging

The following exercise asks you to experiment with different ways of presenting 'dramatic meaning'.

In small groups, chose one of these proverbs.
- Too many cooks spoil the broth.
- A stitch in time saves nine.
- He who laughs last, laughs the longest.
- A fool and his money are soon parted.
- Every cloud has a silver lining.
- Don't count your chickens before they're hatched.
- People in glass houses shouldn't throw stones.
- Still rivers run deep.
- A bird in the hand is worth two in the bush.

Develop a short presentation of the proverb using the following plan.
- Begin by performing the proverb literally. Use freeze-frames, mime, movement, anything to simply communicate the proverb.
- Next, present a brief improvised scene that imaginatively demonstrates the proverb metaphorically. In other words, act out the meaning of the proverb.
- Finish by demonstrating the proverb symbolically. Present an image, a sculpture, a movement or a sound sequence which reflects the meaning of the proverb for your group.

Spend five minutes developing these, then present them to the class. Afterwards, discuss the effectiveness of conveying meaning in these ways.

Navigating Drama

The spine

In our bodies, the spine is the central bone structure from which everything else radiates.

In drama, the spine refers to the central 'dramatic meaning' or message from which everything else radiates. All of the dramatic elements that you choose to use: scenes, dialogue, staging, costuming, sound, lighting, characters and roles must help in communicating your spine to the audience.

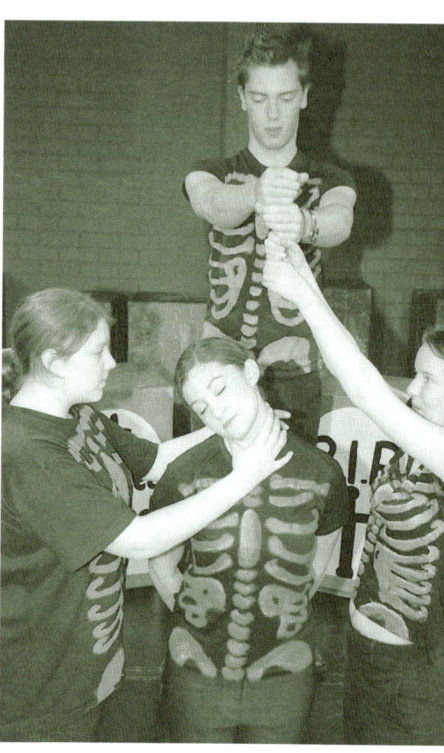

How do you find or decide what the central idea or message is? A useful means of determining the spine of a piece is to ask the following question: *What do we want the audience to think, feel or do as a result of experiencing our piece?*

Your answer to this question will be the basis for your spine.

Of course, some students will answer this question with such things as:

- 'We want the audience to think we are cool.'
- 'We want the audience to enjoy our performance.'
- 'We want to get good marks for our assessment.'.

> **Character:** Representing a three-dimensional character, their particular personality, characteristics and background.

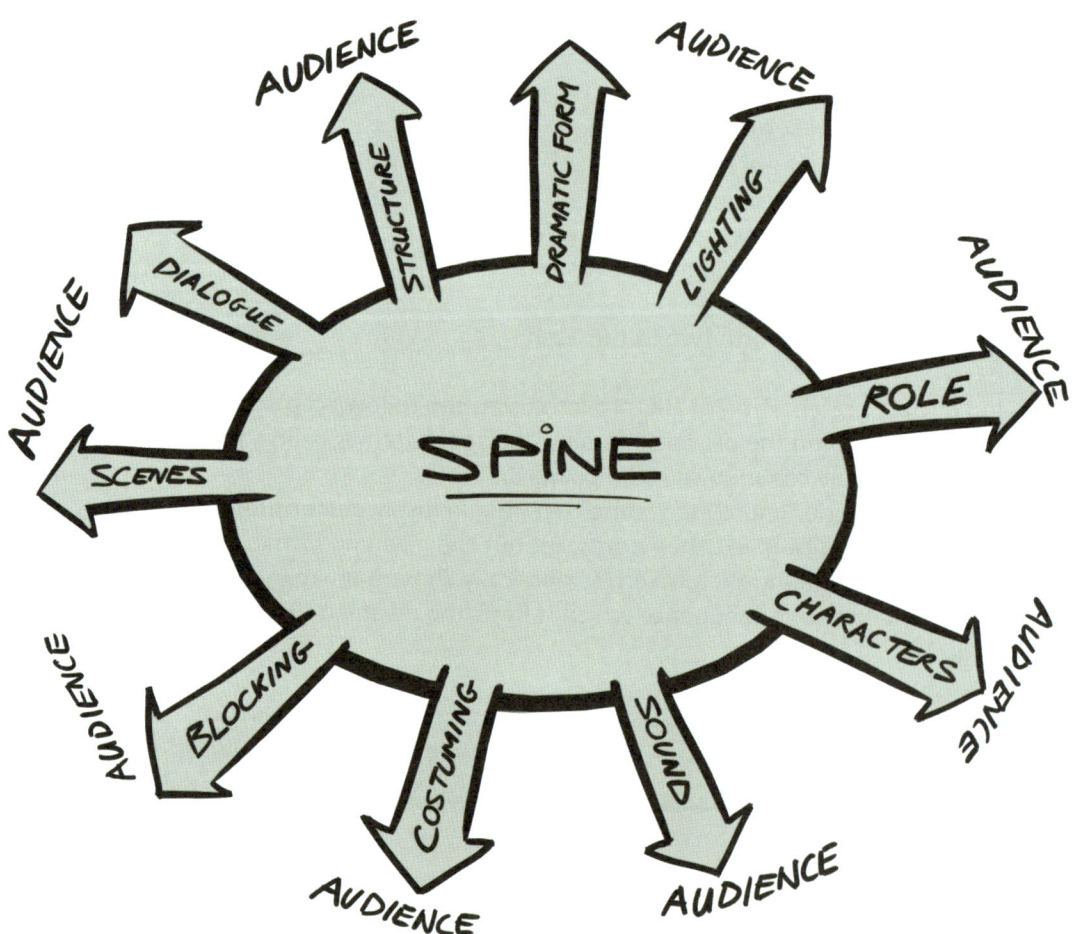

This may be your reason for taking part, but the way to achieve what you want is to choose a spine that reflects the 'dramatic meaning' of your piece – the message. A spine should be an active, positive statement that expresses clearly the group's performance objective. For example:

- 'We want to show the audience how the media presents teenagers as stereotypes'
- 'We want to highlight the problem of poverty in our society'
- 'We want to show how advertising is used to manipulate us into consuming products'.

A spine doesn't have to be profound or earth shattering. A simple spine is effective. But it does need to be clear.

Your topic may not be original, but the way you develop it will be. It will reflect you and your group's own views. It will be unique.

Playbuilding offers new perspectives on old themes.

Once you have a spine you have a strong basis from which to work.

If any scene, sequence, movement, theatrical effect, section of dialogue or piece of staging does not contribute towards conveying your spine to the audience, then it should be omitted, reworked or replaced.

If you have chosen an issue or topic you feel strongly about you will probably be able to come up with an effective spine at the beginning of the playbuilding process. Or you may have selected a general area, for example 'war', but are not yet able to express your point of view clearly. If that is the case, then choose a working spine that expresses your general intention, for example 'war solves nothing'. This can be refined as you work though the process.

Keep testing and revisiting your spine as you work through the development phase of your playbuilding. This process may lead you to a deeper understanding of the topic. Be prepared to adjust any preconceived ideas.

Time spent refining your spine is time well spent. Knowing what you want to say will help you find the best way to say it.

Focus: The performer's focus is creating concentration and belief.

Groups

Playbuilding takes place in groups.

The general principal in drama is that every member of a class should develop skills that enable them to work with anybody else in the group.

Some people only want to work with their friends. This is a trap. They often do what their friends want them to do. A pattern develops. Their performances all start to look the same.

Groups consisting of a mixture of different people usually give the most interesting performances.

If a group member is absent from a playbuilding session, then they must find out what they missed and fit in with any decisions made in their absence.

In any group of human beings there will be

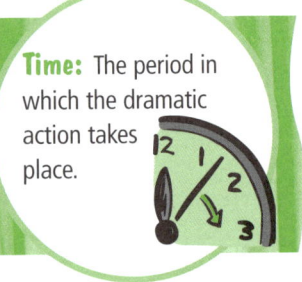

Time: The period in which the dramatic action takes place.

conflict. This is nothing new. There is nothing wrong with disagreement. *The important thing is to listen to other people's points of view and not feel hurt by them.* This is easier said than done. However, it is one of the challenges of playbuilding. A group that is constantly arguing will achieve little.

When you perform on stage you present yourself publicly, and therefore feel vulnerable. It is the same for everyone. Remember, you are not up there by yourself, but as part of a team. Think as a team. Work as a team.

Everybody has their own particular talents and individual perspectives, experiences and opinions. It is your greatest resource in playbuilding. Embrace it.

Forms and structures

Playbuilding can be a difficult process because there are so many options available. Will it be a comedy or a drama? How about something satirical? What sort of situation interests me? Would I like to play someone my own age or someone completely different? What about movement? Music? Mime?

One option of course is to try everything. Who knows? – you might hit on the magic idea that will keep you going to the end. This occasionally happens. But it's rare.

A safer option is to choose a method of working that will allow you to focus your ideas and energy productively, and guide you through the process systematically.

The remainder of this chapter will give you practical experience, and take you through three different approaches to playbuilding. They are:

- narrative playbuilding
- collage playbuilding
- issue-based playbuilding.

Place: The setting of the dramatic action.

Narrative playbuilding

We all enjoy stories. The narrative is the most straightforward form of story telling. We are familiar with it through reading novels and watching films and television. It generally has:

- a beginning, where the characters are introduced and the situation is established
- a middle, where the plot develops and the central conflict is defined
- an end, where there is a dramatic climax and a resolution.

Narrative playbuilding also tells a story.

You can find stories everywhere. Everyone has a story to tell.

You can update old tales and legends. You can also adapt stories from novels, plays, films, songs, poetry and newspaper articles.

Here is the suggested plan of action.

Ten steps to narrative playbuilding

Step 1 Exploring the story
Step 2 Research
Step 3 Finding a spine
Step 4 Working on scenes
Step 5 Working on your performance
Step 6 Putting it together
Step 7 The final script
Step 8 Rehearsing
Step 9 Performance
Step 10 Evaluation

Step 1: Exploring the story

In your groups read this newspaper article.

Dimples a mother never forgot

By JOANN LOVIGLIO AND DAVID RENNIE

Luz Aida Cuevas took one look at the dimpled, dark-haired little girl at a birthday party and instantly knew two things: she was watching her own daughter – presumed killed as a baby in a 1997 fire – and she needed a way to prove it.

So Ms Cuevas pretended the six-year-old girl had gum in her hair, removed five strands from the child's head, folded them in a napkin and put them in a plastic bag.

'Because of TV I knew they needed hair for the DNA', Ms Cuevas said on Tuesday.

The DNA tests confirmed a mother's intuition. The girl was Ms Cuevas's only daughter, Delimar Vera, the girl everyone else believed had perished in a house fire when she was only 10 days old.

Ms Cuevas, 31, never accepted the official verdict that Delimar died in the fire. No human remains were found and an open bedroom window left Ms Cuevas believing her child had been kidnapped. But she could find no evidence until she recognised Delimar at a party in January.

She whispered to her sister, 'Look at her, she's my daughter! I feel it when I see her ... her face and her dimple'.

Carolyn Correa, a cousin of Mr Cuevas, surrendered to police in Philadelphia on Tuesday. She vanished from her home in New Jersey shortly before police arrived to confront her with the results of the DNA tests on the girl she called Aliyah.

Delimar's real mother wept with joy and apprehension as she prepared for a reunion with her long-lost child, who was taken into care while the DNA tests were being carried out.

Police described how Ms Cuevas sat in shock when the results of the final tests were broken.

Ms Cuevas, whose two other children narrowly survived the fire that swept through their two-storey house in northern Philadelphia, said, 'I will go and give her a kiss and a hug and say 'I love you, I love you'. I'm going to spend every minute with my daughter. I'm going to give her a lot of love, hugs and kisses'. Her wish is that in time Delimar will see her as her true mother: 'I hope one day she calls me Mummy'.

Police believe Delimar was hidden in the heart of Philadelphia's close-knit Hispanic community in a shabby house in Willingboro, just across the state line in New Jersey.

Correa, a cousin of the girl's father, Pedro Vera, had been an occasional visitor to Delimar's family home and was there the night Delimar disappeared. She went upstairs to get her handbag and shortly after she left, a fire was discovered in the bedroom where Delimar was sleeping. Experts said the baby's body must have been fully consumed by the fire.

Ms Cuevas and Mr Vera, who have since separated, always had their suspicions about Correa, who stopped visiting shortly after the fire. Mr Vera said: 'I want to see my daughter, talk to her, say, "I'm your father, I love you too much"'.

(Associated Press, The *Telegraph*, London)

First impressions

Spend a few minutes writing down your initial impressions of the story in your logbook. When this is completed, share your thoughts with the others in your group.

Dramatic elements

Now re-read the story. In your logbook, make a note of the dramatic elements of the story. You will need these for reference later on.

Who?	Make a character list. How many characters are there in this story? Record their names if given, and any other information revealed about them.
Where?	In which locations does the story take place?
When?	In what time-frame does the story happen?
What?	Construct a chronology of the events.
Why?	Speculate on the motivation of the main participants of the story. (Why do you think they did what they did?)
How?	How was the deception created and what was done to expose it?
Dramatic tension	Which events contain the potential for dramatic tension for the audience?
Character	Are the characters presented clearly? Can they be developed for performance?
Symbol	Are there opportunities to use symbols to reinforce the meaning of the story?
Language	Are the snippets of the dialogue in the article useable?

Movement: Mood, symbols and motifs can be expressed through realistic or abstract movement.

Brainstorm the story as a group

- What other angles are there to the story?
- What about the child herself? A photograph is included, but how do you think she would react to the situation?
- What about the person who took the child? Why did she do it?
- What about the 'expert evidence' that proved to be wrong?

Dramatic devices

Once you have discussed, collected and recorded your thoughts, make a list of your ideas for turning this story into a theatrical presentation. Consider such dramatic and theatrical devices as:

Narration	An individual narrator? Group narration?
Time and setting	How could you deal with the changes in time and setting?
Character	Multiple role-playing, or individual characters?
Staging	How can you present multiple scenes?
Roles	Individual? Multiple? A mixture of both?
Age	The child ages from ten days old to seven years old, and the other characters vary in age. How will you handle that? Should the child appear in the scene?

Preparation

Each person in the group should choose two to three ideas and do some thinking about how they could be included in the piece. Record these possibilities in your logbook in readiness for Step 4.

The first step is all about getting your ideas going. Don't think you need to come up with the final product now. Record all the ideas contributed – no matter how off-the-wall they may seem. Make sure every group member keeps individual log entries. Restrict this phase of the process to one or two sessions. You need to get on your feet as soon as possible.

Step 2: Research

Compile a list of everything in the article that you need to find more information about. Here are some starting points.
- Can you find any other articles about this event?
- What do you know about the properties of fire? How quickly do houses burn?
- Find out about DNA? What is it? How reliable is it in court cases?
- What are the correct pronunciations of the Spanish names?

Research needs to be done outside of class.

Divide the research among the group and set a time limit for it. Research needs to be done early in the process so that it can be included in your playbuilding. It might help in the acting, planning or staging of your piece. You don't know yet. It might influence the whole direction of your performance.

The amount and type of research depends on the story itself and the knowledge and experience of the group.

Step 3: Finding a spine

What do we want the audience to think, feel or do as a result of experiencing our performance?

Look back over your first impressions of the story. Is there one idea which stands out clearly from the rest? Discuss with the group.

Major themes might be:
- 'A mother's extraordinary intuition in recognising her child'
- 'You don't really know your relatives'
- 'You can't escape your past deeds'
- 'The failure of the legal system and "experts" to determine the truth'
- 'The extraordinary things that happen to people'.

As a group you need to come to an agreement on the spine of your performance. Make a decision.

The next steps are dependent upon it.

If you take the idea that 'the bonds between mother and child' is the dominant theme, then the mother will become the main character.

Structure: The framework through which the content of the drama is presented.

If you decide that the crime aspect of the story is the most important, then the cousin may be the main character.

If you think that the inability of the legal system and the police to discover the truth is the most important theme, then the police and the 'experts' will be featured in your piece.

All of the dramatic elements you choose need to contribute towards communicating your spine to the audience.

If you can't determine an exact spine, decide on a working spine which can be further refined as you work on developing scenes and characters.

Step 4: Working on scenes

Work through the ideas you chose in Step 1.

Start to improvise. (If you're not sure how to proceed, look back at the exercises you completed in Chapter 1: Starting the journey.)

Keep your spine in mind.

Don't forget your research.

Experiment, refine, discuss and select. You may find that some of the ideas that seemed good on paper don't work so well when you are on your feet; in that case, return to the bank of ideas you compiled in Step 1 and try some others.

Make sure you record your work as you go. A good idea is to set aside fifteen minutes at the end of each playbuilding session for documenting the progress of the work in your logbook. It is easier to do this as a group while the events are clear in your head, rather than later on when you may not recall the details.

If a scene is working well and you have decided to keep it, then record it in some detail so that you will have a structure on which to build next time. Record specific lines and particular moves and bits of business. Draw diagrams. This is important. Vague memories are not enough when trying to resurrect a scene from a previous session.

Sessions built on vague memories usually end in despair and an aimless change of direction.

Once you have begun to improvise your ideas, your playbuilding has begun. Productive sessions are when:

- the group members are relaxed
- they have the courage to improvise
- they are working as a team
- they are listening to each other and reacting appropriately
- they have the imaginative ability to be inventive on the spur of the moment
- they are aware of each other so that a central focus is maintained
- they have an understanding of how their character would behave and relate to others
- they are able to create an interesting on-stage conflict.

There are a lot of skills here, and it takes time to learn them. Practice is the key. Some common reasons for sessions not working so well are:
- the group is not working together
- one performer is dominating proceedings
- the plot is unclear
- there is a split focus in scenes
- scenes lack tension or conflict
- there is no ending.

Members of the group are now free to develop their performance from this point. They may wish to scrap the work done in an entire session – but generally this is not a good idea. A new beginning may not necessarily be a better beginning. Fresh starts can become a fruitless habit.

The best advice is to retain at least one thing from each session. It need not be much: a location, a character, a situation, a mood, a theme, a symbol or just one good line. This approach ensures that the development of your group presentation is a creative process rather than just a series of hopeful stabs in the dark.

Step 5: Working on your performance

The playbuilding process is based on collaboration; nevertheless, you will need to demonstrate your performance skills. After all, you will receive an individual mark for your work.

In the group process there is no director to tell you that your voice is too low, that you are not moving cleanly or that your character is not clear. You need to develop the ability to monitor your own work.

- Focus on your character. Do you have a single character or a number of characters to perform? If several, how will you differentiate them?
- Learn your lines early. Get the moves down quickly. This will give you the time you need to concentrate on building belief in your character.
- Complete a character profile and history. How does your character move and speak? How are they different from you? In what ways similar? Allow your character to develop early in the piece.

Moment: The control and manipulation of key moments in the dramatic action.

Step 6: Putting it together

What have you got so far?

By this stage you have probably developed a series of short scenes. They are all on the same topic. Some might be in mime. Others might be comic. Some are working better than others. What happens next?

Now you must build them into a whole.

Wear the director's cap.

If you have a series of short scenes, they should flow easily from one to the next with minimal or no set changes. Look at ways of linking the scenes together so there is no 'dead stage time' where nothing is happening.

Look at the structure of your piece: the order of your scenes. They must tell a story. Use your spine to help you with this. The final moment of the presentation should be carefully chosen and there should be a feeling of completion at the end of the performance.

Give some thought to the look of your presentation. Short scenes are best staged with simple sets. One effective way of doing this is to use a series of boxes which can be arranged in various formations on the stage. They make for quick scene changes. It is unlikely that elaborate sets will be used; they are often not appropriate in playbuilding.

Step 7: The final script

Now is the time to write your final script.

Stop adding new material. There comes a point when creation needs to stop and you must turn your energies towards making the material you have work for you.

Take off the writer's hat and put on the actor's cap.

The director's cap remains on.

Your script should contain the dialogue as well as a description of any non-verbal sequences. It should also show a diagram of the set, with the movements marked in. If you are ill and another performer has to go on for you, they should be able to look at your script and know exactly what to do.

Step 8: Rehearsing

- Drill each scene.
- Look at ways of making the scenes run together smoothly.
- Organise the stage mechanics of entrances and exits.
- Make sure you are working with the actual props and costumes by the final rehearsals. Going on in a performance with a costume you have never worn or a prop you have never touched is asking for trouble.
- Resist the urge to make major changes. Even if you find that some of your choices aren't as effective as you had hoped, look at ways of making them work. Creativity involves more than just choosing the right material; it's also about finding imaginative ways of performing it.
- Drill and rehearse your piece as if it is a published script.
- You need a minimum of three run-throughs – with all props and costumes – to be prepared for your performance.

Sound: The aural devices to enhance performance.

Step 9: Performance

You will learn more about playbuilding in a single performance than if you read every book ever written about it.

Nothing can replace performance experience, or 'flying time'.

Nervous energy affects people in different ways, but if you have worked though the process then you will respond appropriately and cope with whatever happens.

Do a vocal and physical warm-up beforehand. Perform with confidence and enjoy presenting your work to the audience.

Step 10: Evaluation

Evaluation is the most important aspect of the learning process.

Make sure you record your thoughts as soon after the performance as possible – while the experience is still fresh. Don't be too hard on yourself. Look at your strengths and try to be objective. It is quite usual for performers to think that any mistakes or problems in performance were major, when in the audience's mind they were probably insignificant. Don't be afraid to give yourself a pat on the back.

Unit assessment

Making and performing drama: Narrative playbuilding

This project will take three to four weeks to complete.

Conditions
- Work in groups of five to six.
- Use the newspaper article on page 35 as the basis for your playbuilding.
- Apply the ten steps listed on page 35.
- Arrange at least one performance for the school community.
- Time limit of final performance: six to eight minutes.

In your logbook
- Keep a lesson-by-lesson account of your process, for example initial ideas, research, development, visual stimulus, recording of practical sessions, and rehearsals.
- Date all entries.
- After the performance, evaluate your work. What were the strengths and weaknesses of your group playbuilding?

Assessment criteria
- An understanding of how acting and performance techniques are used to communicate dramatic meaning
- Ability to collaborate in the creation and performance of a piece of original theatre
- An understanding of the elements of playbuilding
- Ability to record the process of performance, including visual stimulus and some research

Navigating Drama

Assessment feedback sheet
Narrative playbuilding

———— Level of Achievement ————
Developing   Substantial   Excellent

Performance

	Developing		Substantial		Excellent
Can use acting and performance skills to communicate meaning	1	2	3	4	5
Collaborates in creation and performance of an original piece of theatre	1	2	3	4	5
Understands the elements of playbuilding	1	2	3	4	5

Logbook

	Developing		Substantial		Excellent
Completes entries for each session	1	2	3	4	5
Appropriate research	1	2	3	4	5
Visual stimulus	1	2	3	4	5

Teacher's comments

_____
_____
_____
_____
_____
_____
_____

Student's comments on their strengths, as well as areas that need more work, thought and attention

_____
_____
_____
_____
_____
_____
_____

Collage playbuilding

A collage is any work put together from assembled fragments.

In a collage, different images are juxtaposed to create an overall impression.

The structure of collage playbuilding differs significantly from narrative playbuilding. It is a mix of dramatic and theatrical styles. There is no specific formula. Each scene stands by itself. Every scene is different. Each scene throws a particular light on the topic. The scenes are rather like the facets of a diamond. They are all different yet are all working together. They work on the audience by accumulation.

This form of playbuilding allows the performers to exhibit a range of creative and performance skills. It is also one of the most difficult. You need to be highly imaginative in your choice of topic and selection of material. You must be disciplined and have strong skills in collaboration.

In collage playbuilding, the subject matter or topic you are exploring is the unifying element of the piece. Students have used collage to explore a myriad of topics: art, music, poetry, politics, social manners, relationships, and so on. There is no topic that cannot work effectively.

Here is the suggested plan of action, the ten steps to playbuilding that were outlined in the *Narrative playbuilding* section.

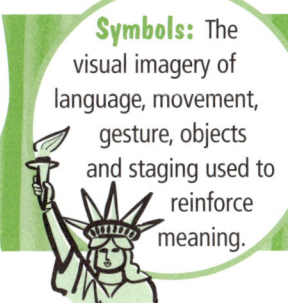

Symbols: The visual imagery of language, movement, gesture, objects and staging used to reinforce meaning.

Step 1: Exploring the topic

Let's take as our topic the environmental subject:

Litter: Cleaning up your act.

First impressions

Spend a few minutes writing down your initial impressions of the topic in your logbook. When this is completed, share your thoughts with the others in your group.

Group brainstorm

Write down a list of all the words, ideas, thoughts, issues, problems, solutions and images related to the topic that occur to your group – no matter how odd. This will become your ideas bank. You can keep coming back to make withdrawals later in the process.

Here is the result of a brainstorming session a group of students came up with on this topic. Steal any ideas from this list and add your own.

rubbish	disinfectant	landfills	packaging
pollution	litter in waterways	recycling	plastic bags
garbage men	gift wrapping	shopping	Super Litter
cans	litter-cam	litter news	litter addict
litter fashion	facts about litter	history of litter	hygiene
prison for litterers	the litter to surf	the litter bug	litter parade
the litterati	a litter TV soap	a litter opera	a litter seeker
the litter police	the litter Top 40	Australian litter idol	litter as art
litter as a team sport	effect on animals	litter puppets	puppy litter
if litter could talk	the litter mermaid	south litter park	litterature
Clean-up Australia	Dave Litterman	Litterers Anonymous	The Litter River Band

Dramatic and theatrical devices

Once you have discussed, collected and recorded your thoughts, make a list of your ideas for turning this topic into a theatrical presentation. Consider the following list of dramatic and theatrical devices.

absurdist	cabaret	caricature	choral work
clowning	comedy	Commedia	dance
documentary	freeze-frames	Greek drama	jingles
masks	medieval drama	melodrama	mime
monologue	montage	movement	musical
opera	physical theatre	poetry	puppetry
reality TV	reenactment	satire	sit-com
slow motion	song	soundscapes	symbolism
theme song	TV advertisements	TV soap	TV news

Rhythm: The manipulation of timing through pace and tempo.

Preparation

Each person in the group should choose two to three ideas and do some thinking about how they could be included in the piece. Record these possibilities in your logbook in readiness for Step 4.

The first step is all about getting your ideas going. Don't think you need to come up with the final product now. Record all the ideas contributed – no matter how off-the-wall they may seem. Make sure every group member keeps individual log entries. Restrict this phase of the process to one or two sessions. You need to get on your feet as soon as possible.

Step 2: Research

This topic is a big one. Because your piece will ultimately be performed for the school community, make the school the centre of your research. Divide the following tasks among the group.

- Find out what effect litter has on the immediate environment, your school.
- How much litter is generated in your school in an average year? How much litter is dropped by any one student on a yearly basis? Work out the amount per day.
- How much money does the school spend on dealing with litter?
- What are the implications for the natural environment?
- Collect some interesting stories.
- Canvas opinions in the local community.
- Look for any articles or studies on litter and littering. Try the internet.
- Why is litter a problem in modern society? Ignorance? Arrogance? Insensitivity?
- Collect some images from magazines that could provide a stimulus for freeze-frames, characters, and attitudes.
- Find out all you can about the Clean up Australia campaign.

Allow enough time to complete the research and bring all the information back to the group to discuss, analyse and incorporate into your playbuilding.

Step 3: Finding a spine

What do we want the audience to think, feel or do as a result of experiencing our performance?

Look back over the notes of your first impressions. Has the group research thrown up any issues, points of view and different angles that could influence your spine? Is there a point of view emerging in the group about what you want to communicate to the audience? Discuss these points:

- Do you think that performing your piece is likely to lead to a reduction in littering?
- What is a reasonable expectation of the effect your message will have on an audience?

It is a worthwhile exercise to heighten awareness of a problem such as littering. It can be achieved by entertaining the audience as well as giving them information.

Keep your spine simple and clear. Positive, active spines work best in playbuilding.

Steps 4–10

The process from this point on is the same as that outlined in *Narrative playbuilding*. Turn back to page 38, and follow through the process from the development of your ideas to the building of them into a final, coherent, dramatic performance.

Atmosphere: The feeling or mood created for the audience.

If you need any help in getting your ideas going, you could stir into your mixture some of the following stimulus material.

Stimulus material
- Take an established plot from literature and adapt it to suit your scene.
- Introduce an object into your scene and allow it to dictate the direction of the action.
- Listen to music; imagine it as the background track to your scene, and take your cue from it.
- Listen to sound effects and let them inspire a fresh scene that might precede or follow yours.
- Steal characters, locations, situations or advertisements from television and rearrange them to suit your scene.
- Take a character from history, literature, or someone you saw on the train, and introduce them into your scene.
- Play with different styles of theatre, reworking your scene as pantomime, mime, Shakespearian drama or television soap.
- Play with different genres, reworking your scene as science fiction, crime, historical romance, or fantasy.
- Include a movement section, a song or a dance routine.

Unit assessment

Making and performing drama: Collage playbuilding
This project will take three to four weeks to complete.

Conditions
- Work in groups of four to five.
- Use the topic 'Litter: Cleaning up your act' as the stimulus for your playbuilding, or, if you are familiar with collage, you could choose your own topic.
- Apply the ten steps listed on page 35.
- Arrange at least one performance for the school community.
- Time limit of final performance: eight to ten minutes.

In your logbook
- Keep a lesson-by-lesson account of your process: initial ideas, research, development, visual stimulus, recording of practical sessions, and rehearsals.
- Date all entries.
- After the performance, evaluate your work. What were the strengths and weaknesses of your group playbuilding.

Assessment criteria
- Uses acting and performance techniques to communicate dramatic meaning
- Ability to collaborate in the creation and performance of a piece of original theatre
- An understanding of the elements of playbuilding, stagecraft and production
- Ability to record and evaluate the process of rehearsal and performance

Assessment feedback sheet

Collage playbuilding

	Level of Achievement		
	Developing	Substantial	Excellent

Performance

	Developing		Substantial		Excellent
Can use acting and performance skills to communicate meaning	1	2	3	4	5
Collaborates in creation and performance of an original piece of theatre	1	2	3	4	5
Can manipulate the elements of playbuilding	1	2	3	4	5
Understands the elements of stagecraft and production	1	2	3	4	5

Logbook

	Developing		Substantial		Excellent
Completes entries for each session	1	2	3	4	5
Appropriate research	1	2	3	4	5
Visual stimulus	1	2	3	4	5
Post-performance self-evaluation	1	2	3	4	5

Teacher's comments

_____
_____
_____
_____

Student's comments on their strengths, as well as areas that need more work, thought and attention

_____
_____
_____
_____
_____
_____

Issue-based playbuilding

Issue-based playbuilding is a form of collage playbuilding, only with a strong political or social message. It is an umbrella term for political, protest or documentary playbuilding.

Political theatre is didactic; it wants to educate you about the broad political picture.

Protest theatre is more concerned with a specific issue.

Documentary theatre uses historical records, verbatim accounts, newspapers and interviews to explore social and political issues.

Issue-based playbuilding is concerned with bringing the audience's attention to a particular issue. It may explore a current political issue in a satirical fashion to highlight a particular point of view. It may investigate a historical event to make the audience see it in a different light. It may point out the absurdity of particular social behaviour. In this form of playbuilding it is not just a good idea to have something to say about an issue – it is compulsory.

Playwrights with a political message

The playwright Henrik Ibsen, who wrote in the late 1800s, is considered the father of modern drama. His plays are about social and political issues. He writes about suicide, corruption in local government, human delusions, and the nature of marriage. *A Doll's House*, his most famous play, explores the issue of a women's role in society. When first performed, it shocked the audience. Ibsen presented his ideas in the form of a *naturalistic* play.

In the middle of the 1900s, the German playwright Bertolt Brecht developed a different dramatic form – *epic theatre* – to present political issues. He set his plays in the past so his audience could objectively study the events. He used popular fairground music and songs to interrupt the action. He did not want his audience to become emotionally involved in the play. He wanted them to be *intellectually involved* with the issue. To reinforce this, he had his actors enter through the audience, step out of character, swap roles, and break into song. He wanted the mechanics of the performance to be exposed to the audience. Sets were changed in full view of the audience. Signs told the audience what was about to happen. Narrators stepped in and out of the story. Sets and props were symbolic, and the lighting simple.

Dario Fo is a modern Italian playwright who uses popular, grotesque comedy to attack issues such as police violence, inflation, political corruption and exploitation of workers. He uses a mixture of farce, clowning, *Commedia dell'Arte*, slapstick and physical theatre to get his political messages across.

Augusto Boal is a Brazilian theatre practitioner who developed a form of theatre called the 'Theatre of the Oppressed', in which the spectators become 'spec-actors'. They join in the action on stage, contribute ideas, take over roles, and use the situation to explore issues such as racism and unemployment.

These playwrights were all concerned with bringing about political and social change. You may wish to explore some of their methods in your playbuilding.

> **Language:** The verbal and non-verbal forms in which the dramatic action is conveyed.

Chapter 2 Navigating playbuilding

If you have already gained experience completing *Narrative playbuilding* and *Collage playbuilding,* you may feel confident enough to navigate your own way through *Issue-based playbuilding*. Alternatively you might like to follow the ten steps to playbuilding outlined in the *Narrative playbuilding* section.

Step 1: Exploring the issue

Let's take as our topic the social issue:

'The more advanced technology becomes, the less humans are able to communicate'.

First impressions

Spend a few minutes writing down your initial impressions of the issue in your logbook. When this is completed, share your thoughts with the others in the group.

Group brainstorm

Write out a list of all the words, ideas, thoughts, problems and solutions related to the issue.

Here are some ideas to get you going.
- A company in America is offering a service where you pay them to break off with your girlfriend or boyfriend by SMS.
- Office workers communicate with their co-workers by email, even when they are sitting beside each other.
- In an average lifetime we will have to use and remember over 2000 passwords and pin numbers.
- Banks want us to pay a fee if we want to be served by a human being.

Some relevant words and phrases

sms	mobile phones	cameras	computers
cyber reality	ear phones	chat rooms	email
modems	floppy discs	addiction	agoraphobia
laptop	ipod	alarms	electronic organizer
phone bills	generation gap	feelies	reality TV
r u o k	bionic man	robots	voice recognition
spam	computer geeks	surveillance	handwriting
voicemail	internet	leisure	net nanny
DVD	internet fridge	wired	cyber-relationships
answering machines	computer speak	CD	plasma

Dramatic and theatrical devices

Once you have discussed and recorded your thoughts, make a list of your ideas for turning this issue into a theatrical presentation. Consider the following dramatic and theatrical devices.

absurdist	anti-climax	asides	Boal
Brechtian	cabaret	caricature	choral work
clowning	comedy	*Commedia*	dance
Dario Fo	direct address	disguise	documentary
farce	focus	freeze-frames	flashbacks
gibberish	Greek drama	historical	imagery
jingles	juxtaposition	language	links
masks	medieval drama	melodrama	mime
monologue	montage	motif	movement
musical	narration	opera	pace
physical theatre	poetry jingles	puppetry	reality TV
re-enactment	satire	sit-com	slapstick
slow motion	song	soundscapes	stillness
structure	symbolism	tempo rhythm	theme song
TV advertisements	TV current affairs	TV soap	TV news

Preparation

Each person in the group should choose two to three ideas and do some thinking about how they could be included in the piece. Record these possibilities in your logbook in readiness for Step 4.

Step 2: Research

This topic is large; technology affects many areas of our lives. Try to find a range of views. Come up with research ideas of your own. Here are some starting points.
- Canvas different opinions on the issue.
- Find relevant articles in newspapers or on the internet.
- Find out more about Brecht, Dario Fo and Augusto Boal and apply their techniques to your playbuilding.

Allow enough time to complete the research and bring all the information back to the group to discuss, analyse and incorporate into your playbuilding.

Step 3: Finding a spine

What do we want the audience to think, feel or do as a result of experiencing our performance?

Look back over the notes of your first impressions. Has the group research thrown up any issues, points of view and different angles that could influence your spine? Is there a point of view emerging in the group about what you want to communicate to the audience? Discuss the following points.
- Is our society developing technology for its own sake?
- Are human beings social animals who need interaction with each other to live healthy lives?
- Are disproportionate amounts of our taxes being spent on developing technology at the expense of basic social welfare, health and education?
- Is technology the cure for all our ills?
- Is technology controlling us or are we controlling it?
  Keep your spine simple and clear.

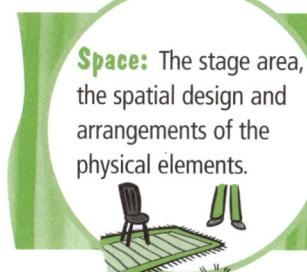

Space: The stage area, the spatial design and arrangements of the physical elements.

Steps 4–10

The process from this point on is the same as that outlined in *Narrative playbuilding*. Turn back to page 38 and follow through the process from the development of your ideas to the building of them into a final, coherent, dramatic performance.

There will be moments in the development of your playbuilding piece when you will come up against a brick wall. As a group you might have tried hard with a particular scene but it has died on you – you are no longer able to squeeze any life out

of it. The moment will come with no warning. It will not necessarily appear early in the development of the work. It might come some time after the work has begun – and just when you thought everything was going well.

Do not despair.

You have in fact arrived at a block which all creative people experience at some time. The answer does not lie in forcing the issue – nor does it lie in giving up.

It lies in making a lateral jump.

The lateral jump

A lateral jump is a sideways move. It is a creative act. It is a fresh vision, leading to a new direction.

Consider one or more of the following lateral jumps as a possible cure for a scene that seems to have run out of inspiration.

- A comedy might easily be turned into a drama (or a farce, pantomime or piece of absurd theatre) with little alteration to plot or characters.
- A male character might be turned into a female character (and vice versa).
- Two actors might swap roles.
- A scripted scene might work better as mime.
- A realistic script might be changed into one where the dialogue is disjointed, consisting of half-sentences, unfinished lines or single words.
- A mime might be more effective when performed in slow motion.
- Two separate scenes might work well if played simultaneously.
- The order of scenes might be changed; a play might work better if the scenes are performed in exactly the reverse order.
- A scripted scene might be turned into a dance routine, while retaining the dialogue.
- A scene might be saved by adding (or subtracting) music, a song, or sound effects.
- Symbolic costume and make-up might replace realistic costume and make-up.
- An insignificant aspect of a scene might be elevated into the central focus of the scene.

> **Audience Engagement:** The ultimate purpose of all elements of the dramatic action.

Unit assessment

Making and performing drama: Issue-based playbuilding

This project will take three to four weeks to complete.

Conditions

- Work in groups of three to four.
- Use this statement as your stimulus: 'The more advanced technology becomes, the less humans are able to communicate'.
- Apply the ten steps listed on page 35.
- Arrange at least one performance for the school community.
- Time limit of final performance: ten to twelve minutes.

In your logbook

- Keep a lesson-by-lesson account of your process: initial ideas, research, development, visual stimulus, recording of practical sessions, and rehearsals.
- Date all entries.
- After the performance, evaluate your work. What were the strengths and weaknesses of your group playbuilding?

Assessment criteria

- Can select, order and manipulate acting and performance techniques to communicate dramatic meaning
- Collaborates in the creation and performance of a piece of original theatre
- Demonstrates an understanding of the elements of playbuilding
- Can manipulate the elements of stagecraft and production
- Can record, analyse and evaluate in depth their own work and the group's work

Navigating Drama

Assessment feedback sheet
Issue-based playbuilding

	Level of Achievement		
	Developing	Substantial	Excellent

Performance

Can use acting and performance skills to communicate meaning	1	2	3	4	5
Collaborates in creation and performance of an original piece of theatre	1	2	3	4	5
Understands and manipulates the elements of playbuilding	1	2	3	4	5
Understands and manipulates the elements of stagecraft and production	1	2	3	4	5

Logbook

Complete and comprehensive entries reflecting your process	1	2	3	4	5
Post-performance analysis and self-evaluation	1	2	3	4	5

Teacher's comments

_____
_____
_____
_____
_____
_____
_____

Student's comments on their strengths, as well as areas that need more work, thought and attention

_____
_____
_____
_____
_____
_____
_____

Part Two

Dramatic Contexts

Chapter 3

Commedia dell'Arte

Outcomes

In this topic you will:

- develop an understanding of the conventions of *Commedia*

- develop a *Commedia* character using appropriate voice and physicality

- learn and apply knowledge of *Commedia* in performance

- record the process of rehearsal and performance.

Background

Commedia dell'Arte means 'comedy of professional craftsmen'.

Commedia was outdoor theatre. A troupe of actors would arrive in town, set up their stage in a central place, and attract an audience with clowns, mime artists and mountebanks. When an audience had collected, they would perform their play.

It is a comic, boisterous and irreverent form of theatre.

From about 1550 to 1750 the *Commedia* became enormously popular and spread from Italy across Europe. In England it influenced Shakespeare's comedies. In France it influenced Molière. Even today, we see its influence in puppet shows, pantomime, stand-up comedy, early silent film and the mardi gras.

It began in Italy sometime in the middle of the 1500s. It probably developed from entertainments put on by quacks, magicians and mountebanks as they shouted their wares to the crowds in market places ('mountebank' means: 'someone who stands on a wooden stage'). When a crowd had gathered, the performer and their assistants would entertain the audience, and this would lead to a smart sale and the crowd parting with its money!

This kind of outdoor entertainment still takes place, with jugglers, acrobats, fire-eaters, musicians and still-life artists entertaining crowds in market places, parks and harbour-sides today. Onlookers throw money.

Another source of the *Commedia* was the carnival. The carnival originated in Roman times, and celebrated the beginning of spring: the death of the old year and the birth of the new. At carnival time people wore masks which freed them from their usual social behaviour, and all kinds of wild practices took place. Octavio Paz wrote: 'Anything is permitted. Men disguise themselves as women, gentlemen as slaves, the poor as rich. The army, the law and the clergy are ridiculed'. This desire to wear a mask, dress up, mimic other people, and laugh at the rich and powerful lies at the heart of all improvised comedy.

A mountebank selling his wares in a market place.

The elements of Commedia

Commedia is improvised theatre. There are no scripts.

Commedia is essentially visual theatre and its characteristics are simple:
- stereotypical characters
- comic stage routines
- music and dance
- variations on a simple plot.

Commedia belongs to the actors. It is one of the few types of theatre controlled by actors, and not by playwrights, directors or theatre managers.

The actors wore masks and each performer played only one role. So, for example, a particular actor would play Arlecchino in every play. He would come to know his character very well.

Commedia actors worked from brief plot summaries known as *scenarios*. The plays were all much the same – variations on a basic storyline: a rich miser (Pantalone) wants to marry his beautiful daughter (Isabella) to a wealthy nobleman (Il Capitano or Il Dottore). The nobleman is ugly and proud, and the girl is in love with someone else (Flavio). Servants (Arlecchino, Colombina, Brighella) are sent to carry messages between all the parties involved. They lose the messages, deliver them to the wrong people, or fall in love with the young lovers themselves! A sad, mute servant (Pedrolino) pines for Colombina. The play ends with everyone getting what they deserve.

As the *Commedia* developed, many new characters made their appearance, but the nine mentioned above are the best known. These are stock characters, each with their own mask and costume, stance, walk, gesture and voice. Each one is also associated with a domestic animal.

Into this loose storyline of pompous old men, vain lovers and wily servants, the actors added their own comic routines. These consisted of lazzi (sight gags), concetti (comic monologues), and burle (double act routines). Actors developed their own routines and techniques and guarded them safely. Swordfighting, acrobatics, music and dance were also important elements of the *Commedia:* the old men, the young lovers and the zanni.

The characters

In *Commedia*, the characters are stock characters; that is, they are always the same. The Italian audiences would know who each one was as soon as they came on stage – even if they were in disguise, which they frequently were.

There are three types of characters in *Commedia:* the old men, the young lovers and the *zanni*.

1 The old men

The best known of these are *Pantalone*, *Il Dottore* and *Il Capitano*, though Il Capitano is younger than the other two. These men come from a wealthy social class. They are usually miserly, sick and stupid, and are portrayed as figures of fun. They are grumpy characters. They see themselves as chick-magnets, which is funny because they are *old* and clearly past it. The audience loves it when their plans go wrong and they are tricked out of their money, or when their marriage to a girl young enough to be their daughter fails to take place.

Pantalone is a high-status character. He has bags of money. He is powerful. He tells everyone what to do. Pantalone is a thin man who wears red trousers, a red cap and yellow slippers. He also wears a long black cloak. His mask has a long, hooked nose, and bushy eyebrows. His props are a medallion hanging around his neck, and a moneybag hanging at his crotch. Pantalone crouches, knees bent, leaning forward, protecting with his hands the two most important things in his life! He walks with small steps, like a chicken, and he speaks with a chicken-like squawk. He is mean to his servants, grovels to Il Dottore and lusts after Colombina. He is so concerned with his own plans that he does not notice the audience.

Il Dottore is a doctor. He is a high-status character. He is extremely fat. He dresses completely in black, even wearing a black skull-cap. He carries a white handkerchief. His mask consists of a bulbous nose; thick, white eyebrows; and cheeks reddened by drink. His animal is a pig. He walks around in circles using tiny steps, leaning backwards, belly sticking out before him, swinging his arms around and pontificating on any subject under the sun. He speaks a load of rubbish, and considers himself an authority on everything. He only notices the audience when he needs them for one of his lectures. He is Pantalone's friend, because Pantalone is rich.

Il Capitano is an impostor. He pretends to be a captain in the army, and therefore a high-status character. He wears huge boots and a ridiculous army uniform. He carries a long sword, and struts about the stage with large strides, a straight back, and his nose in the air. He speaks in a loud, deep voice. He constantly stops before the audience and salutes them, expecting admiration. He is a parody of a bold military man. When he sees a cockroach he is frightened and tries to kill it. He fails. When chased by a mouse he can only run on the spot, yelling at the top of his voice. The audience enjoys his final humiliation.

2 The young lovers

The young lovers are young and attractive. They are the children of aristocrats, and have names like *Isabella* and *Flavio*. Their costumes are highly fashionable. The young lovers do not wear masks, but their overdone make-up has the same effect as a mask. They wear wigs, mascara and beauty spots (the men as well as the women). The men carry handkerchiefs, and the women carry fans. They love the idea of being in love, of looking beautiful, and they are infatuated with the person they see in the mirror. They check themselves in mirrors all the time. They are vain and self-centred, but not vicious. They prance about the stage like spoilt, silly children playing at being the world's greatest lovers. They pant like little dogs and teeter around the stage like ballerinas. Sometimes they flirt with a member of the audience. They have little or no physical contact with each other.

3 The zanni

The *zanni* developed from low-class immigrants who made their way to the large Italian cities. They were rough, tough characters. They did what had to be done to earn a living: selling food and drink, carrying goods and working in the markets. In *Commedia* the best known of these characters are *Arlecchino, Colombina, Brighella,* and *Pedrolino*.

Arlecchino is usually a servant to one of the old men. He is usually in love with Colombina. Like all *zanni* he is a low-status character. He is recognised by his costume of green, red and white triangles. He wears a black hat. His animal is a cat. He moves like a cat. Although he is agile, he is not too bright. His plans seldom work out. His disguises often come unstuck. Colombina does not always repay his attentions. Arlecchino's prop is a slapstick, a stick with a flap attached to it so that it makes a loud noise when he is beating someone with it. He reacts to everything – including the audience.

Colombina is usually Isabella's maid. She wears a dress with a low neckline, an apron and a cap. Like all *Commedia* women she wears full make-up but no mask. The presentation of Colombina depends a bit on the actor playing the role. Sometimes she is coy and feminine, and her animal is a dove. Other versions present her as feisty and sexy, and her animal is a heifer. She is always intelligent. She knows everything that is going on. She loves gossip, and speaks in a lively, cheerful fashion. She rests her hands on her hips or throws them up in the air. She is an affectionate woman, and all the men are attracted to her. She flirts with the audience too, showing that she knows, with them, how stupid men really are.

Brighella is the top *zanni*. He is usually Pantalone's servant. He is Arlecchino's friend, but he is more intelligent than Arlecchino. Brighella is clever, witty and cunning. He is a thief, a cheat and a liar. He has no conscience. His animal is a rat. He will try anything as long as it is at someone else's expense, gives him a laugh or makes him rich. Brighella sets the *Commedia* plots going. His mask is green, with a hooked nose and thick lips. His clothes and cap are white with green borders to them. He wears a purse and a dagger. He moves all the time. He walks like a frog. He is a cynical character who confides his diabolical plans in the audience.

Pedrolino is the only male *zanni* who does not wear a mask, yet his white face and black eyes gives the impression of a mask. He is childlike, innocent, and in some cases mute. He is a bit of a loner. He is faithful to Colombina, but she does not return his love. His master, Il Dottore, is jealous of his natural sensibilities, and treats him badly. Pedrolino does not have the characteristics of a particular animal. He is the most human of the *Commedia* characters. He wears baggy white clothes and a pointy white hat. He is a sad character, but the audience identifies with him and warms to him.

Pedrolino developed over time into the character Pierrot, and is the precursor of the Marcel Marceau's white-faced clown.

You should be able to recognise these characters now. See if you can put names to the illustrations of the characters on the following two pages.

Navigating Drama

Chapter 3 Commedia dell'Arte

6

7

8

9

Stagecraft

Appreciating drama: Character research

Using the internet, your library and the knowledge you have gained so far, copy this *Commedia* character chart into your logbook and complete it. A useful source is John Rudlin's book *Commedia dell'Arte – An Actor's Handbook*. This chart should now be used as the basis for your work in the practical performance tasks.

Name and status	Costume and mask	Props	Animal	Characteristics	Stance and walk	Speech	Relationships
Pantalone (Old Man)							
Il Dottore (Old Man)							
Il Capitano (Old Man)							
Isabella (lover)							
Flavio (lover)							
Arlecchino (*zanni*)							
Colombina (*zanni*)							
Brighella (*zanni*)							
Pedrolino (*zanni*)							

The mask

The *Commedia* mask is really only a half-mask, covering the top half of the face. The mouth and chin are not covered. All the *Commedia* characters, except the young lovers, the women and Pedrolino, wear masks; in the case of these characters their thick make-up has the same effect as a mask.

The masks represent types, not individuals. The characters are two-dimensional, cartoon characters. We recognise them. The vain old miser, the self-absorbed lovers and the cunning servants are all well known to us.

The mask reflects human qualities such as greed (Pantalone) and sadness (Pedrolino). Animal qualities are also evident in the masks, for example Pantalone looks, and therefore moves and speaks, like a chicken. Il Dottore is a pig, and Brighella is a rat.

In *Commedia*, there is no complex characterisation, no tragedy, no character development and no psychological realism.

Just basic comedy.

Commedia acting is ensemble acting.

When acting in a mask the actor has to surrender to the mask. They have to stop 'acting' and let the mask do the work. Actors must combine gesture and movement to allow the mask to come alive. They must learn a whole new body language. They must learn whole new speech patterns.

Chapter 3 Commedia dell'Arte

Stagecraft

Making drama: Making a mask

The first thing you should do is make your own mask. Originally masks were made of leather, but that is impractical. Try papier mache rather than plaster. Papier mache is lighter, less messy, and less likely to crack.

As each *Commedia* actor played only one role, you might like to choose a *Commedia* character for yourself*. You will need to do a bit of research first to find out the details of your mask.

Probably the easiest way to construct a mask is to buy a cheap plastic see-through mask from a toy shop or theatre shop. Cut away the section below the mouth. You can now build your papier mache mask onto this base. Glue small squares of newspaper onto the base, and then build it up from there. Make it fairly strong. Construct the individual contours of the face with extra papier mache strips, lengthening the nose and adding the warts where necessary. Make two holes at either side. Wait for the mask to dry, then remove the base. Attach elastic through the holes to hold it in place.

Paint it. It should now be ready to use.

* You might like to retain this one character for the entire unit. Remember that, because of the masks, it is easy in *Commedia* for girls to play the male roles.

Navigating Drama

On Your Feet

Commedia: Workshop 1

Warm-up
This game starts off a session with energy and humour, and helps performers get to know each other quickly.

Confusion bingo
Sit in a circle with a pencil and a copy of the bingo sheet below. On a given command enter the circle and attempt to fulfil all the requests on the sheet. Each completed exercise must be witnessed and signed off. Vary your partners. The idea is to see who can complete the challenges first. Continue until everyone has finished.

Attracting an audience
Since *Commedia* had its origins in market place behaviour, you might like to try a bit of fairground spruiking. You will need a strong voice for this, and a sense of what might entertain a crowd.

Imagine that you are in a market place in the sixteenth century. You are trying to attract an audience. You are one of the following:
- a priest threatening hell fire
- an inventor selling a new invention (make one up)
- a quack selling cure-all medicines
- a magician, juggler or snake charmer.

Get someone to lift you off the ground for five seconds. They initial here:	Have a mock sword-fight with someone for a whole minute. They initial here:	Exchange a piece of clothing with someone. They initial here:	Find four people to play 'ring-a-ring-o-rosie'. They initial here:
Get someone to watch you run on the spot for 15 seconds. They initial here:	Tell someone you love them in a long passionate speech. They initial here:	Get someone to watch you walk like a duck. They initial here:	Hug someone of the same sex. They initial here:
Get two people to listen to you laugh like an idiot for a whole minute. They initial here:	Get someone to do an impersonation of a well-known personality. They initial here:	Find someone with a birthday this month. They initial here:	Touch someone who is not part of this game. They initial here:
Hug someone of the opposite sex. They initial here:	Wheelbarrow someone across the room. They initial here:	Get someone to listen to you squawk like a chicken. They initial here:	Collect five initials from people who have not yet signed your sheet. They initial here:

On Your Feet (continued)

Go about your business. Create your patter. Sell your wares. It is a good idea for two or three mountebanks to work side by side and see who can pull in the crowd. The crowd, of course, is the rest of the group. Play fair.

Character work

These exercises introduce students to the Commedia characters.

Working with animals

Most of the *Commedia* characters have clear animal qualities. The animals were always domestic animals. Try the following.

- Select one of the following: chicken (Pantalone), pig (Il Dottore), peacock (Il Capitano), love bird (Isabella), cat (Arlecchino), heifer (Colombina) or rat (Brighella).
- First: move around the room as your chosen animal. No sound. Use your whole body. First of all, mime the animal, and then gradually transform yourself into the relevant *Commedia* character while retaining the dominant animal movements.
- Next: work in pairs. Sit at a table. Each actor must choose a different animal. First, make the farmyard noises of your chosen animal, taking it in turns to cluck like a chicken or snort like a pig. Then, gradually, without losing the basic animal sounds, begin to form words and have a conversation. Improvise a short scene. You might find that the animal sounds start to inform your posture and gestures as well.
- Continue the above scene by getting up from the table and moving around the room. Turn your conversation into an argument. Retain your animal-like voice as you add movement to the act.

Making a face

In *Commedia*, the mask dictates everything. The actor must subordinate themselves to the gaze of the mask. The following exercise asks students to focus on the mask.

Sit in front of a mirror and make faces. Explore your face and see what it can do. Screw it up. Distort it. Select an extreme expression that you like. Take some tin-foil and push it around the contours of your face, making a quick mask of your expression. Take it off and study it. With a couple of holes and a piece of string, fix the mask to your face. Now experiment with ways of bringing this fixed mask to life. Move around the room. You are going to have to find a body language that can give life to your mask.

Finally, you might like to introduce your character to the rest of the group. If you can't think of anything for your character to say, you might like to try *grummelot*. *Grummelot* is a *Commedia* technique whereby a character gabbles off a series of sounds that convey a sense of character but are in fact pure nonsense!

Using your mask

It is now time for you to use the mask you made earlier. Actors must learn to know their own mask well, and understand its particular power.

Two actors stand at opposite sides of a room, like cowboys ready for a shootout. Lean over and look down at your mask, face to face, holding it at arm's length. Study it. Then, still leaning forward, slip the mask over your face. As you straighten up and face the other actor, let the mask take over. Do not think what to say. Do not plan anything.

Together, improvise a scene in character.

Navigating Drama

Stagecraft

Appreciating drama: Workshop summary

Here is a summary of what was learned in the workshop.
Make a record in your logbook.
- Voice and movement are very important when performing *Commedia*.
- Actors must combine gesture, movement and voice to allow the mask to come alive. They must learn a whole new body language.
- *Commedia* is ensemble acting. There is no room here for the selfish performer.

Now, in your logbook, describe the workshop from your point of view. As you do so, answer the following questions.
- Which tasks did you feel most comfortable doing, and why?
- Which tasks did you find more difficult? State why.
- As an actor, what skills have you learnt so far from working in *Commedia*?

The acting style

Commedia is a highly energetic form of theatre.

In *Commedia*, all the characters speak in loud voices, unless they are doing a 'stage whisper'. This is partly because of their market place beginnings. The theatrical reason is that these are extreme characters, and they need to present themselves in an extreme way. If they speak in their natural voices they lose their punch and are just not funny.

Wearing a mask changes everything for an actor.

Gestures become larger than usual and slower than is natural.

We like to act naturally today, but that's not the way to present *Commedia*. For example, we might think that it's perfectly reasonable to scratch one's face during a play, but if the face is a mask, then that is a crime. To touch the mask takes away its magic.

Again, we like to face the person we are talking to. It's our natural way of communication. But think about it. Who wants to see the side view of two masks? The power of the mask, its 'gaze', comes from its full frontal view. The 'eye' of the mask is situated at the end of the nose. So actors in the *Commedia* must face the audience when speaking. They only turn to watch the other actor reply.

As most of the scenes in *Commedia* are either two-character scenes or three-character scenes, this is not so confusing as you might expect. In *Commedia*, the entire cast does not come onto the stage together until the final scene when the lovers are united, the old men are humiliated, and all is resolved.

In *Commedia*, the characters are on the move most of the time. Even in their curtain-call they bob and wave like animated puppets. If they were to remain still and take a normal curtain-call the magical energy would drain out of the performance.

There are moments of stillness, however. One thing a *Commedia* actor must learn to do is stare at the audience with a fixed gaze for many seconds. It's a cartoon effect. If this happens after an energetic piece of business, it will get a laugh.

Commedia is about opposites.

One thing you will have noticed about the *Commedia* characters is that each contains a paradox. Each character believes they are one thing, but in fact they are the complete opposite. These characters have no self-knowledge. For example, Pantalone likes to think of himself as being attractive to women but in fact when he does manage to snare a young woman he is unable to keep up with her as he is too old and slow!

Stagecraft

Appreciating and making drama:
The paradox of character

Copy this chart into your logbook, and fill in the paradoxes of character that exist in each of the main characters. Pantalone and Il Dottore have been done for you. In each case suggest a comic routine that might illustrate the paradox.

	The image	**The reality**	**Comic routine**
Pantalone	Pantalone thinks of himself as being attractive to the fairer sex.	His body is not able to keep up with his desires.	Pantalone offers Colombina a gold coin. He suggests that she first sits on his knee. She does. He goes to embrace her, but she slips out of his clutches. She escapes. Pantalone chases her, but she tricks him at each turn. He eventually stops, helpless, puffing and panting. She takes the coin and goes.
Il Dottore	Il Dottore presents himself as a clever man with a broad general knowledge.	He is an ignoramus who speaks a load of rubbish.	Il Dottore arrives at the bedside of a sick man. He pontificates about the causes of the illness, ignoring the patient and using long words. The patient gets bored, gets up and makes himself a cup of tea.
Il Capitano			
Isabella			
Flavio			
Arlecchino			
Colombina			
Brighella			
Pedrolino			

Commedia actors are also asked to perform two contradictory actions at the same time. This is because the *Commedia* mask has a life of its own and often acts independently of the body. An example of this is when Arlecchino is summoned by his master: his body has to answer the call but his eyes remain fixed on the sexy Colombina! It's not easy. The *Commedia* actor has to develop a flexible neck.

Another example of this is when Il Capitano is being chased by a mouse: he runs on the spot and the audience sees his legs moving very fast from the side view while his mask faces them and is completely still. Put a bit of music to this and you have a classic cartoon effect.

Music has always been a component of *Commedia*. Most of the *zanni* carried instruments and they used them constantly to underline the action.

Comedy is also created by a sudden change of mood or pace. Someone who is happy might suddenly start bawling (Isabella, Flavio). Someone who is sad might suddenly break into a dance (Pedrolino). Someone who has been lecturing everybody for hours might suddenly stop (Il Dottore). Someone who has been asleep at work might suddenly wake up and indulge in a flurry of stupid activity (Arlecchino). This is always funny, and is a key element of *Commedia*.

There is nothing politically correct about the *Commedia*. People constantly hit each other, steal from each other and trick each other. They make fun of foreigners and old people. They hurt animals. They make bum jokes, boob jokes and fart jokes. Low-brow humour prevails. What did you expect? It's slapstick!

The lazzi

The *lazzi* (singular: *lazzo*) are comic routines which have nothing to do with the plot of the play, but which were inserted into the action by the actors whenever they thought the show needed some variety or comic relief.

These routines were developed and polished by the performers themselves. It is interesting to see how this might have happened. Here is a modern example. Half way through a recent student *Commedia* production a mobile phone went off in the audience. People shuffled in their seats. Arlecchino and Colombina were on stage at the time. Acting in character, Arlecchino pulled out his slapstick, held it up to his ear and said 'Hello'. The audience enjoyed the moment. After the show the actor playing Arlecchino said that he could have taken the joke a stage further. He could have said something like, 'Mabel, I've told you not to phone me at work'.

Colombina said she would be suspicious and would grab for the phone. 'Who is it?'

'It's my bank manager.'

'No, it's not.'

A chase around the stage would follow, with Colombina finally tripping Arlecchino, sitting on him and taking the phone, only to find that the batteries had run out! Our two actors rehearsed this routine, and had it ready in case they were interrupted by another mobile phone the next night!

By the way, do not worry about Mabel and the bank manager. Topical allusion is a main source of humour in the *Commedia*. It is a *lazzo* in its own right.

Lazzi, then, are basically visual gags although many of them contain dialogue. The catch phrase is itself a *lazzo*. *Lazzi* have usually been well rehearsed. They sit at the back of a performer's mind, and can be used when called for.

There are many kinds of *lazzi*. Arlecchino often performs acrobatic *lazzi*, such as falling over a piece of furniture into a bathtub. It takes skill to do this without getting hurt. Many *lazzi* involve violence. A favourite is when Il Capitano comes along to stop two people from fighting, only to receive the blows himself. There are food *lazzi* and acrobatic *lazzi*, *lazzi* where characters dress up as other people, and just plain stupid *lazzi*.

Lazzo of the Tooth Extractor: Il Dottore and Arlecchino fool Pantalone (centre) believing that rotten teeth are causing his bad breath. Using oversized or ridiculous tools, they extract some of Pantalone's good teeth!

On Your Feet

Commedia: Workshop 2

Concentration exercises

Students of Commedia need a high degree of concentration; they must be able to respond quickly to different situations on stage.

Breakfast

Find a space in the room, sit down and mime eating your breakfast. Decide what you are having for breakfast, and where each object is on the table in front of you. Do not hurry. Just have breakfast. Eat. Drink. Read the papers. Do not talk. Remember – you have just got up.

A few students will move around the room trying to break your concentration by using any method at all (other than touching). If you laugh or make eye contact, you are out. See who can retain the strongest concentration.

Soap box

Sit in pairs, facing each other, with legs outstretched and feet touching. Each person must select a topic. Both participants must then talk about their topic at the same time – without faltering, pausing, grinning or giving up. See if you can both keep talking fluently for a full minute or more.

Seconds delay

Sit in pairs facing each other with legs outstretched and feet touching. One participant delivers a lecture on any topic. The other has to repeat the speech, word for word, after a half second's delay (like the echo you sometimes get on a long-distance phone call). See if you can both keep talking fluently for a full minute or more.

On Your Feet (continued)

Applause

Sit in a large circle. Each student has a number: 1, 2, 3, 4. Someone stands in the middle of the circle and counts slowly. Clap when your number comes up. If your number is a multiple of the number being counted, clap again. Concentrate.

Movement

Here are some basic movement exercises to help actors forget the natural way of acting and embrace the exaggerated behaviour of Commedia *characters.*

Walk the walk

Walk around the room. Lead with your chin, groin, shoulder or chest. What differences of character do these induce?

Walk around the room. Adopt different heights. Be thin and tall, short and squat, bend your knees, or stick out your bum. What differences of character do these induce?

Walk around the room. Move in different ways: point, thrust, glide, swish, stride and push. What differences in character do these induce?

Walk around the room as a *Commedia* character. Take turns in imitating: the chicken walk (Pantalone), the fat man waddle (Il Dottore), the army stride (Il Capitano), the balletic teeter (Isabella, Flavio), the feline glide (Arlecchino), the sly slope (Brighella), the sexy swish (Colombina), and the sad shuffle (Pedrolino).

The Mask

Mask work

These exercises help the Commedia *actor understand the role of the mask.*

Prepare to use your mask. Lean over and stare hard at your mask, face to face, until you get a strong sense of character. Study it hard. Then slip it on. The female characters, who do not have masks, should study their overly made-up mask-like features in a mirror in the same way.

In pairs, act out an argument between Arlecchino and Colombina, or Pantalone and Isabella. First, play the scene naturally, each person looking at the other. Next, play the scene out to the front, presenting the audience with the full face of the mask when you speak. Discuss your findings.

The *Commedia* mask often acts independently of the body. Stand behind a pillar. Keep your body out of sight. At the same time, move your head out sideways from the pillar to the left and to the right as if spying on someone. The important thing is to keep the head vertical and the eyes horizontal. Take care not to strain your neck.

Stand sideways to the audience and run fast on the spot. Arms and legs should pump furiously. As you do this keep your face perfectly still and turned towards the audience.

Lazzi for one

Here are some *lazzi* that require only one actor. Work up your own mime routine. Wear your mask. You will notice that the humour relies on your being able to contrast two opposite moods or actions. Finally, present your work to the rest of the group.

Mime. You are Pantalone. You are shuffling down a street ogling the girls. You react to a few beauties. You try a few quick moves without success. Be inventive. Finally, walk into a lamp post.

Mime. You are Il Dottore. You are examining a body on the table in front of you. You open the body, cut the veins, staunch the blood, take out some tubing. Make your actions clear. Be inventive. Finally, drop a chicken sandwich into the body, lose it, and sew up the body.

Mime. You are Il Capitano. You strut and parade around, saluting and giving a macho performance. You see a mouse and panic. You try to kill it, and fail. Be inventive. It runs up your trouser leg. You run on the spot, lifting your legs high and screaming like a baby.

On Your Feet (continued)

Mime. You are Isabella or Flavio. You are spending a lot of time at your mirror. You add a beauty spot, smile, worry about the size of your bum, become happy with it, try to adjust a physical feature without success, smile, kiss your reflection. Be inventive. Finally, you open a beauty box – which explodes white powder all over you.

Mime. You are Arlecchino. You tread on some chewing gum. You try to remove it in a number of ways, each one getting you into more of a mess than before. Make your actions clear, even acrobatic. Be inventive. Finally, eat it.

Mime. You are Colombina. You are supposed to be doing the housework for Pantalone but are much more interested in gossiping on the phone. Make your actions clear. Be inventive. Finally, Pantalone enters. He sees you talking on the phone. Slowly, try to hide. End with frozen smile.

Mime. You are Brighella. You are jumping and hopping about, desperately looking for a toilet. Be inventive. Finally, you can't wait any longer. With your back to the audience you unzip your trousers. As you do so you become slowly aware of the audience behind you. React.

Mime. You are Pedrolino. You enter the bathroom, turn on the shower, prepare to take off your clothes, notice the audience, turn your back modestly, undress, get into the shower, sing, shower, get out, towel yourself dry, put on underarm deodorant, get dressed, check your breath, do your teeth, comb your hair, look at yourself in the mirror, leave your house, pick flowers, moonwalk to Colombina's house, holding flowers out before you, and knock at her door. She opens the door and slaps you in the face.

Lazzi for two

Spend some time working in pairs on these *lazzi*. As many *lazzi* are intrinsically vulgar, be sensitive when preparing your work. Most of these *lazzi* involve some dialogue. Finally, wearing masks, present your work to the rest of the group.

Scenario. Pantalone is talking to Il Capitano (or Il Dottore) about a young girl he has met. Il Capitano is interested and takes out his sword showing how he would defend her honour and fight off all suitors. He has trouble with his sword. He drops it. He cuts himself. He misses the sheath and sticks it down his trousers. Pantalone tries to help. Be inventive. Finally, the girl walks past and both men bump into each other and fall down while attempting to follow her.

Scenario. Isabella and Flavio are looking for each other, but are so self-absorbed that they keep missing each other. When one enters the stage, the other exits. They call out love messages to each other. When one calls, the other misjudges the direction. When one looks up, the other looks down. Be inventive. Finally, they back into each other, turn around and receive the shock of their lives!

Scenario. Arlecchino has come to attend to the plumbing (or painting or window cleaning) at Colombina's house. He finds himself very attracted to her. He makes all sorts of amorous gestures behind her back, yet each time she turns around he pretends to be busy at his work. Be inventive. He turns each gesture into a moment of plumbing (or whatever).

Scenario. Brighella seems unwell. He is lying on the ground, arms and legs splayed out like a starfish. His left arm, however, is sticking up. Pedrolino approaches, wanting to help. He slowly pushes down Brighella's left arm only to see his right leg rise up. He reacts. Next he pushes down the leg. An arm rises. Speed it up. Be inventive. Finally, Pedrolino kneels over Brighella's right leg. He smiles innocently at the audience, who knows what is going to happen. He pushes down the left arm, and the right leg rises up sharply! End with Pedrolino's frozen stare out into the audience.

On Your Feet (continued)

Lazzi for three

Spend some time working in groups on these *lazzi*. You will have to decide how to get the most laughs out of each situation. Be inventive. Decide, also, how you will conclude each *lazzo*. Rehearse your work thoroughly before presenting it, in masks, before the rest of the group.

Scenario. Flavio and Isabella are having a lovers' tiff. Il Capitano tries to come between them to stop the fighting. The lovers are so absorbed in their row that they do not notice him. Their anger increases, and Il Capitano ends up bruised and battered on the floor. Still without noticing him, they make up.

Scenario. Colombina is in love with Brighella but is married to Arlecchino. She pretends to be sick. Brighella pretends to be a doctor. When Arlecchino is on stage, Brighella attends to Colombina in a very doctor-like fashion, but when Arlecchino is off-stage or not looking, Brighella's moves are distinctly non-medical.

Scenario. Pantalone has given Il Dottore some money to put on a horse named Hottentot (or any name, though it is better to pick one that can be broken down into shorter words). Il Dottore has spent the money on drink. Pantalone, suspecting this, confronts Il Dottore angrily. He wants to know where his money is. Il Dottore's says he gave it to his servant Pedrolino to put on the horse. Pedrolino is passing by, and Pantalone turns to ask him if this is true. Pedrolino, loyal and innocent, nods. Pantalone asks him for the name of the horse. Standing behind Pantalone, Il Dottore mimes 'hot' for Hottentot. Pedrolino interprets it as 'sexy'. As Pantalone gets more and more angry, Il Dottore's mimes become increasingly manic and Pedrolino's interpretations crazier by the minute.

Stagecraft

Appreciating drama: Workshop summary

Here is a summary of what was learnt in the workshop.
Make a record in your logbook.
- In *Commedia*, actors must respond physically to different musical cues.
- When acting in a mask, the actor must surrender to the mask.
- The actor should face the audience when speaking in a mask, rather than looking at the person they are speaking to.
- The 'eye' of the mask is situated at the end of the nose.
- Performing *Commedia* is an exacting physical task, often requiring an actor to do two different things at the same time.

Now, in your logbook, describe the workshop from your point of view. As you do so, answer the following questions.
- Which *lazzo* did you feel most comfortable doing, and why?
- Which aspects of the *lazzi* did you find more difficult? State why.
- As an actor, what skills can you take from the *Commedia* and use when playing more mainline theatre?

The concetti

The *concetti* are comic monologues. All the *Commedia* actors would have their own *concetti* ready for use at some time during the play. This would provide a break in the action, and give each character a chance to present themselves to the audience.

Stagecraft
Making and performing drama: Writing a concetti

In your logbook, write a *concetti* for one of the *Commedia* characters. You may choose to develop one of the ideas below, or you could compose a *concetti* of your own.

CHARACTER	CONCETTI
Pantalone:	A long complaint about the cost of living and how you can't trust anyone these days because they are all out to cheat you of your money
Il Dottore:	A tedious medical diagnosis full of jargon and Latin words which, if acted upon, would kill a man in minutes
Il Capitano:	A pompous, completely unbelievable, not to say physically impossible, account of his remarkable feats of war
Isabella and Flavio:	A soppy speech worshipping the magical and levitational effects of being in love
Arlecchino:	A despairing monologue running through a range of suicidal alternatives now Colombina has rejected him
Colombina:	A female tirade about the inequality of the sexes in all things social, financial and sexual
Brighella:	A recruiting drive for the army; mentioning all the underhand incentives needed to entice lazy and devious conscripts
Pedrolino:	A gentle observation illustrating his simple, uneducated, ill-informed – yet thoroughly wise – view of life

Learn your monologue by heart and present it, wearing the mask, to the rest of the group.

Do not forget to move in character.

The burle

The *burle* are comic routines which take place between two characters. Like the *lazzi* and the *concetti*, the *burle* were well rehearsed and would be inserted into the action where appropriate. The nearest thing we have to the *burle* today are the two-person comedy routines – you might have heard of Laurel and Hardy, or Kath and Kim. One is usually the 'straight' character, the other is the comic, though this is not always the case. Sometimes both are funny. Many comedians find it easier to work in pairs.

Navigating Drama

Stagecraft

Making drama: Improvising a burle

You may like to start by viewing an old Laurel and Hardy routine, or watching a comedy team from a recent television show.

Work in pairs. Improvise a *burle*. The best effects are obtained by just getting up and doing it. Take the risk. Before you begin, however, it is a good idea to be sure of your character and of your character's attitude to life. You may adopt the attitude of a *Commedia* character if you wish, or you may invent your own.

In *Commedia*, each character carried a prop, and this was sometimes used as the trigger for a routine. Ladders were popular. So were buckets, swords, sacks and piles of plates. You could adopt that idea.

Other basic *burle* situations are:
- one character recounts a childhood event (or an adventure) while the other constantly interrupts with stupid questions
- the two characters pretend to be authorities on some technical subject they know nothing about
- both characters try to outdo each other when recounting their exploits with the opposite sex.

Take a few minutes to decide on your characters and set up the basic situation. Then improvise your *burle* before the rest of the group.

Kath and Kim do comic routines like the *burle*.

The script

There are no scripts in *Commedia*.

The actors knew the basic plot of the play, which was usually in three acts. There were many scenes to each act, and these were listed in the scenario, which was posted up backstage before the show. The scenario gave a brief run-down of each scene. For example:

Scene one: Arlecchino, Colombina and Il Capitano

1 Arlecchino and his wife Colombina enter, both complaining about the hardships of married life. Both think they have got the rough end of the deal. Arlecchino says Colombina was lucky to snare him. She runs through a list of his shortcomings. He finds excuses for all of them. Finally, he has had enough.
2 He chases her, threatening terrible things if he catches her.
3 Her screams bring Il Capitano, who tries to stop the fight. Colombina tells Il Capitano to mind his own business. She says she likes being chased. Il Capitano apologises and then tells Arlecchino to continue chasing Colombina. Arlecchino says he'll chase his wife when he wants to, not when told to by Il Capitano.
4 Arlecchino and Colombina then both chase Il Capitano off stage.

That Scoundrel Scapin

Someone who was greatly influenced by the *Commedia* was the French playwright Molière. His plots follow the *Commedia* plots, and his characters are based on the *Commedia* characters. If we want to get an idea of how a *Commedia* scene played, we need look no further than Molière. Here is a scene from his play *That Scoundrel Scapin*. Molière's original names have been changed to the *Commedia* equivalent.

Brighella: (*pretending not to notice Pantalone's entry*) O Lord! What a disgraceful thing to happen! It's the father I feel sorry for! Poor old Pantalone, what will he do?
Pantalone: (*aside*) What's he saying about me with a face as long as a fiddle?
Brighella: Can't anyone tell me where Mr Pantalone is?
Pantalone: What's the matter, Brighella?
Brighella: I've looked everywhere for him, but not a chance.
Pantalone: Here I am.
Brighella: (*still pretending*) He must have hidden himself somewhere no one would ever think of looking.
Pantalone: Hey! Are you blind? I'm here.
Brighella: Oh, Sir, I couldn't find you anywhere.
Pantalone: I've been standing under your nose for the last hour. What's the matter then?
Brighella: Sir ...

Pantalone: What?
Brighella: Sir, your son ...
Pantalone: My son what?
Brighella: Has had the most incredible bad luck imaginable.
Pantalone: How?
Brighella: I came across him a little while back terribly upset by something, I don't know what, that you had said to him. We went for a walk down to the harbour, to try and cheer him up. There, among other things, we noticed a Ruritanian yacht, beautifully equipped. A handsome young Ruritanian invited us on board and it was handshakes all around. Once we were aboard it was kindness itself – gave us a buffet lunch with excellent fruit and choice wines.
Pantalone: What's so terrible about that?
Brighella: Wait a minute, Sir, we're coming to it. While we were eating, the yacht put to sea, and, once outside territorial waters, the Ruritanian put me in the tender and sent me to tell you that if you don't send me back at once with five hundred guineas he'll make your son work his passage to Africa.
Pantalone: What the devil! Five hundred guineas!
Brighella: Yes, Sir, and what's more, he only gave me two hours.
Pantalone: Grrr ... Ruddy Ruritanian! He's trying to bleed me white!
Brighella: It's up to you, Sir. Quick, think of some way of saving your son. I know how deep your affection is for him.
Pantalone: What the devil was he doing on the yacht?
Brighella: He had no idea what would happen.
Pantalone: Off you go, Brighella, and tell this Ruritanian I'll have the police on him.
Brighella: The police on the high seas? You must be joking.
Pantalone: What the devil was he doing on the yacht?
Brighella: It must have been his unlucky day.
Pantalone: Brighella, the situation demands that you act like a loyal servant.
Brighella: Yes, Sir.
Pantalone: Go and tell this Ruritanian to send my son back, and you stay in his place until I've got the ransom money together.
Brighella: Eh? Do you realise what you're saying? Do you think this Ruritanian is so daft as to take a miserable wretch like me in place of your son?
Pantalone: What the devil was he doing on the yacht?
Brighella: He couldn't guess what was going to happen. Remember, Sir, he's only given me two hours.
Pantalone: You say he wants ...
Brighella: Five hundred guineas.
Pantalone: Five hundred guineas! Has he no moral standards?
Brighella: Yes Sir, his morals are standard – for a Ruritanian.
Pantalone: Does he know how much five hundred guineas is?
Brighella: Yes Sir, he knows it's five hundred pounds plus five hundred shillings.

Pantalone:	Does this cheapskate think five hundred guineas can be found just like that?
Brighella:	These people don't listen to reason.
Pantalone:	But what the devil was he doing on the yacht?
Brighella:	It's unfortunate, but there you are! You can't foresee these things. Please Sir, hurry up.
Pantalone:	Here, take the key to my desk.
Brighella:	Right.
Pantalone:	Open it.
Brighella:	Fine.
Pantalone:	In the left-hand drawer you'll find a big key which opens the attic door.
Brighella:	Yes.
Pantalone:	Take all the old clothes in the big trunk and sell them to the pawnbroker to ransom my son.
Brighella:	*(giving back the key)* Eh? Are you crazy, Sir? I wouldn't get five pounds for that lot, and what's more, you know how little time they've given me.
Pantalone:	What the devil was he doing on the yacht?
Brighella:	Oh, save your breath! Forget about the yacht and remember that time's short and that you're in danger of losing your son. Oh, poor young master, I may never see you again. Even as I speak you're being carried off to Africa! But God is my witness that I did all I could for you, and if you don't get ransomed you've only a hard-hearted father to blame.
Pantalone:	Wait Brighella, I'll go and fetch my money.
Brighella:	Hurry then Sir. I'm terrified in case the clock sounds the hour.
Pantalone:	Four hundred, did you say?
Brighella:	Five hundred.
Pantalone:	Five hundred pounds?
Brighella:	Guineas.
Pantalone:	What the devil was he doing on the yacht?
Brighella:	Yes indeed, but hurry.
Pantalone:	Why didn't he go for a walk somewhere else?
Brighella:	That's true, but be quick!
Pantalone:	Oh, that confounded yacht!
Brighella:	*(aside)* The yacht's got him, good and proper.
Pantalone:	Here, Brighella, I've just remembered that I was on my way to the bank with exactly that sum. *(holding out his wallet)* Here, go and ransom my son.
Brighella:	*(holding out his hand)* Very good, Sir.

Navigating Drama

Stagecraft

Performing drama: Performing a Commedia scene

Work in pairs. Your challenge is to get as many laughs as possible from a performance of this scene from *That Scoundrel Scapin*. Use masks. Think about character and movement. Consider the use of props. Learn the lines and perform the scene to the rest of the group.

The stage

When the *Commedia* troupe first arrived in town, the actors would parade through the streets advertising their play. This carnival procession would include music and dancing, and would attract young and old. The actors would talk to the townsfolk to gather some local jokes and topical allusions to include in their show.

Then the players would set up their stage.

The site for the stage had to be carefully chosen. A large area such as a market place was suitable. It was a good idea to place the stage opposite some buildings, to give the actors' voices more resonance. They also had to make sure that the sun was not in the audience's eyes.

Song and dance in *Commedia*. Two actors rehearsing in front of a portable *Commedia* stage.

Chapter 3 Commedia dell'Arte

Stagecraft

Appreciating drama: The Commedia stage

Incorporate the following statistics into a drawing of a *Commedia* stage. Draw a front view, a cutaway side view and a bird's-eye view. Label your drawings. Work in your logbook.

The Commedia stage
- a raised platform 150–200cm high
- stage area not too large
- width was more important than depth
- a curtain roughly 250cm high ran along the back of the stage; it had an opening in the centre for entrances and exits
- slits or windows in the curtain for characters to spy through
- a stepladder behind the curtain for characters to climb up and peer over the top
- characters could also enter and exit at the sides of the stage
- a curtained-off backstage area for actors to change

Stagecraft

Appreciating drama: Some questions

Answer these questions in your logbook:
1 Why do you think a market place was a good place to set up a *Commedia* stage?
2 Why do you think a *Commedia* stage did not need much depth to it? Consider the use of masks in your answer.
3 What were some of the problems a *Commedia* actor had when leaving the stage?

Stagecraft

Appreciating drama: When the Commedia came to town

Imagine that you are a teenager living in a small Italian town in the year 1600. Using your imagination, as well as the knowledge you have gained, describe the day the *Commedia* came to town.

Write in your logbook. Do not fill your work with lists of facts. Try to capture something of the excitement of the day and the flavour of the *Commedia* performance.

Unit assessment

Performing drama: Performing a Commedia scene

(Six to eight lessons' preparation.)

Here are three scenes from different *Commedia* scenarios.

Depending on the character you have developed, choose the appropriate scene and, as a group, prepare it for performance. You must perform in costume and wearing your mask. Your work must include:

- a *lazzo*
- a *concetto* or *burle*
- a song, dance or piece of live music.

Scenario 1. Isabella sits at a window, looking beautiful and sighing over Flavio. Her father Pantalone appears at the door saying, 'I have brought you your future husband'. She turns excitedly, only to see Il Capitano drooling over her. Isabella tries to talk her father out of the marriage, saying things like, 'I am too young', but Pantalone will not change his mind. So Isabella plays along with him, at the same time making her distaste for Il Capitano very obvious.

Scenario 2. Flavio is in bed, lovesick. He sends his servant Brighella to fetch a doctor, and to convey a love note to Isabella. Il Dottore arrives, slightly drunk. He starts examining Flavio. When Brighella returns, Il Dottore bundles him out of the room, saying it is a quarantine area. Brighella returns, dressed as a doctor, wearing exactly the same clothes as Il Dottore. He then joins in the examination – at the same time delivering Isabella's reply in secret.

Scenario 3. Pedrolino sits alone. Colombina enters with bucket and mop to clean the room. Pedrolino leaps up and willingly helps her with all her chores. Arlecchino enters, gives Colombina a rose, and entertains her with his acrobatic skills. Pedrolino sees this and goes off to find a rose. Arlecchino and Colombina flirt together, in the process upsetting the bucket and messing up the room. Arlecchino exits. Pedrolino enters with a wilting rose and offers it to Colombina. She refuses it and follows Arlecchino off stage. Pedrolino is sad, then suddenly happy.

In your logbook

- Keep lesson-by-lesson entries, recording your process.
- Afterwards, include a self-assessment evaluating the degree of success in presenting the scene.

Assessment criteria

- Knowledge and understanding of the elements of *Commedia*
- Use of voice and physicality in presenting character
- Ability to engage with an audience in a way that is appropriate to the style
- Ability to record and evaluate the process of rehearsal and performance

Assessment feedback sheet

Performing a Commedia scene

	Level of Achievement		
	Developing	Substantial	Excellent

Performance

Use of voice and physicality in creating character	1	2	3	4	5
Ability to perform in mask	1	2	3	4	5
Ability to engage the audience	1	2	3	4	5

Logbook

Completes entries for each rehearsal	1	2	3	4	5
Post-performance self-evaluation	1	2	3	4	5

Teacher's comments

_____
_____
_____
_____
_____
_____
_____

Student's comments on their strengths, as well as areas that need more work, thought and attention

_____
_____
_____
_____
_____
_____
_____

Chapter 4

Melodrama

Outcomes

In this topic you will:

- develop a character using gestures and physical stylisation
- learn and apply knowledge of melodrama in performance
- record and analyse the process of rehearsal and performance
- evaluate the influence of melodrama in contemporary performance.

Background

Melodrama flourished in the 1800s. As a form of theatre, however, it has a bad name today. To call someone 'melodramatic', especially a performer, is an insult. The modern taste is for a more realistic and natural style of acting. The exaggerated gestures and grand vocal techniques used in melodrama seem comic to us; however, in its day this type of theatre attracted larger audiences than in any other period in the history of western drama. The average city-dweller in the nineteenth century attended the theatre regularly – each week, according to some historians. The average Australian city-dweller today attends the theatre once a year. Theatre audiences in the nineteenth century were very familiar with the theatrical conventions of the period, and they knew what they wanted. They wanted thrills, spectacle, and sensation.

The elements of melodrama

In the nineteenth century, melodrama did not mean 'over the top' or 'excessively dramatic'. Look at the word again and see if you can discover an alternative meaning.

MELO *drama*

That's it! *Melo* is drawn from melody. Music. Originally, 'melodrama' simply meant 'drama with music'.

Melodrama is essentially visual theatre, and its characteristics are simple:
- stereotypical characters
- sensational stage effects
- plot contrivances with virtue triumphing over vice, and plot dominating characterisation.

Within this basic structure various types of melodrama evolved: domestic melodrama, nautical melodrama, military melodrama, temperance and gambling melodrama, canine melodrama and factory melodrama.

The stock characters – the Hero, Heroine, Villain, Male Servant, Soubrette (female servant), Old Man and Old Woman – developed variously within these forms. The Hero and Heroine were, of course, good; the Villain was evil. The Male and Female Servants were there for comic relief. The Old Man and the Old Woman were generally good people.

Music was a vital part of the theatrical experience.

Although the golden age of melodrama was in the late 1800s, many of its theatrical devices and conventions are familiar to us today. If you watch television, you are already well on the way to being an expert in melodrama. If you go to the movies, you are already familiar with many of the conventions of melodrama.

When movies began in the early 1900s they were silent. The acting style that was used in early film relied on physical gesture and facial expression to convey meaning; and music was used in much the same way as it was in melodrama:

- to heighten audience emotion
- to establish character
- to telegraph plot or character information
- to create dramatic climaxes and
- to keep the audience interested.

Sometimes the use of music could be excessive. Jerome K. Jerome, describing a performance in 1880, remarked:

Nearly all the performers had a bar of music to bring them on each time, and another to take them off; a bar when they sat down, and a bar when they got up again, while it took a small overture to get them across the stage. As for the leading lady, every mortal thing she did or said, from remarking that the snow was cold, in the first act, to fancying she saw her mother and then dying in the last, was preceded by a regular concert.

The role of music changed as the century progressed; as well as heightening the drama, it came to be used as a signaling device for the audience, directing their attention to specific points and telegraphing plot. No longer was music subsidiary to the drama. It had become part of it.

Stagecraft

Appreciating drama: Drama with music today

Today music plays a major role in movies. The horror movie, for example, relies heavily on music to involve and scare the audience. In this genre, a common device is to establish an insistent rhythm in the music, mimicking the human heart rate. If this rhythm is slowly increased, your heart rate slowly increases, making you feel really scared and apprehensive.

The following task requires you to watch a movie or television program of your own choice, and study how music is used to manipulate the audience.

In your logbook, divide a full page into two columns as shown on the following page. In the first column, number and record each time music is used in the film. In the second column, try to describe what dramatic function the music is serving, or what it is trying to get the audience to think or feel.

Use of music	Purpose
1 Opening credits	Grabs audience attention and establishes time and mood.
2 Scene 1	Creates link between credits and first scene.

You may find it useful to refer to the following list.
Music is used to:
- heighten emotion
- establish character
- create tension
- create a feeling of apprehension
- underpin action
- heighten humour
- telegraph action
- guide audience attention
- establish change of time or place.

When you have filled one page you should have enough examples to form an opinion about the debt that modern film and television owe to melodrama.

Tableaux

A tableau is a frozen stage picture.

It is a theatrical device that was used in melodrama, usually at the end of an act, to create a theatrical climax. It would summarise what had just happened, and would highlight or resolve the conflict. Often there was no dramatic climax in the writing of melodramas, in which case tableaux were used to end a scene in an exciting manner.

Stagecraft

Making drama: Tableau

This illustration depicts the tableau at the end of Act 1 of a famous domestic melodrama, *East Lynne*. In groups of five, improvise the scene leading up to this moment. Base your impro on the characters and situation apparent in the tableau.

Lady Isabel's flight in *East Lynne*.

The acting style

For melodrama the acting style was physical and highly stylised. Actors' movements were large, overblown and generous. Their voices were loud, clear and overstated.

Why?

In the nineteenth century the theatres were big. They had to be to contain their audiences. There was no means of amplifying sound in these buildings, so the actors had to find ways of conveying their performances to all areas of the theatre. They had to be able to project their voices over a relatively long distance and still be understood. Articulation needed to be highly developed. Added to this was an important fact: the majority of the audience was illiterate. They could not read. So you couldn't necessarily rely on words alone to convey the story. The actors also needed to be good at non-verbal communication.

The acting style of melodrama conformed to a code. Meaning was conveyed to the audience through stance and gesture. Look at the following six illustrations. Who are they, and what can you deduce about the characters from their physicality?

Navigating Drama

In melodrama, specific stances and gestures would signal particular emotions. The actors were obliged to use this code. Acting manuals from the period contain rigid directions for the portrayal of each emotion.

A hand to the forehead indicated suffering.

A hand over the heart indicated virtue, honesty and faithfulness.

A hand to the eyes indicated tears.

A downcast head indicated defeat. And so on.

In melodrama, an actor wasn't asked to experience a particular feeling, they were expected to indicate the feeling to the audience. The audience expected this style of acting. If an actor attempted anything different, they would be boo-ed and hooted off the stage.

Stock characters were the norm in melodrama. These were two-dimensional characters. The Hero, Heroine, Villain, Male Servant, Soubrette, Old Man and Old Woman were stereotypes that audiences recognised. (The soubrette was the equivalent of Colombina in the *Commedia*). They expected these characters to be present in every play.

The code dictated the costuming. The Hero was dressed in white. The Villain was dressed in black. The comic Male Servant wore a checked vest and jacket, and so on. The Hero would often wear a military uniform, or, in a nautical melodrama, a sailor's uniform. A costume of rags and patches would indicate moral collapse.

Voices also had to conform to the rules. The Hero had to be a tenor; the Villain a deep base. The Heroine was a light soprano, the Soubrette a mezzo, and so on.

Make-up was not a feature until later in the century with the advent of electric lighting in theatres. The combination of gas or oil lighting and heavy make-up produced too much distortion for make-up to assist in establishing character.

Stagecraft

Appreciating drama: The acting code

Using the knowledge you have gained so far, and with a bit of additional research, copy this melodrama character chart into your logbook and complete it. This chart should be used as the basis for your work in the practical performance tasks.

Character	Dominant emotion	Voice	Costume	Colour	Range of gestures
Hero					
Heroine					
Villain					
Male Servant					
Soubrette					
Old Man					
Old Woman					

On Your Feet

Melodrama Workshop 1

Warm-up
A strong flexible voice is mandatory for melodrama.

Breath
Stand with your feet as wide apart as your hips. Hands on your lower belly. Breathe in slowly to a count of five. Hold for five. Exhale for five. Repeat until you have established a relaxed rhythm. Gradually increase to a count of ten. Then fifteen.

Vowel sounds
Run through the following vowel sounds and project your voice to the opposite wall: ah, eh, ee, i, o, oo. Now whisper the sounds. Add consonants to the vowel sounds and run through the alphabet starting with ba, beh, bee, bi, bo, boo alternating between projecting and whispering.

Mexican wave
Controlling your body is equally important. Standing in a circle, send a Mexican wave in slow motion around the circle. Add a facial expression to the movement. Each person creates a different physical and facial movement to send around the circle.

Slo-mo spine roll
Beginning with hands stretched straight up, slowly curl your body towards the floor, beginning with the fingers, then hands, lower arms, shoulders, head, chest. Bend at the knees and hang for a count of fifteen, then reverse the process. Repeat three times.

Body messages
In melodrama, the actor's physicality conveys more meaning to the audience than the dialogue. Try the following exercise and ban all words for the duration.

Communicate without words
Individual students communicate the following directions to the group without using words.

- Run.
- Stop.
- Hide.
- Laugh.
- Sleep.
- Freeze.

Now progress to more complicated directions.
- Do five push-ups.
- Come here and help me.
- What did you watch on TV last night?
- Do you want fries with that?

Students can now create their own tasks for the class to decipher and complete.

Discuss the problems encountered when words can't help you. How were the messages conveyed?

Freeze-frames
Freeze-frames are a theatrical device which were used in melodrama. They were called tableaux and were employed at the end of each act to provide a climax, resolve a plot, or telegraph a plot development.

- Work in small groups.
- Each group is given a caption.
- The groups are to use these as the stimulus for three freeze-frames in which they explore or expand on the caption. Try the following list.
  - learning to drive
  - hunger
  - the winning goal
  - the verdict
  - loss
  - pity
- Take ten minutes to create your three tableaux. Drill them several times, and then present them to the rest of the group. Afterwards, discuss the effectiveness of clean and clear physicality, mentioning character, tension, focus, and layers of conflict.

On **Your Feet** (continued)

- In bigger groups, construct a larger scale freeze-frame inspired by a recent public event. Work to include different levels of conflict. After presenting the tableaux, discuss their effectiveness as a device for conveying dramatic meaning.

Word and gesture

In melodrama you act with your whole body. Every feeling or gesture has to be readable for an audience. Some people find it easy to physicalise as they talk; others don't. The following exercise focuses on gesture.

- This is a game that requires each participant to produce a physical gesture for every word that is spoken. If you speak a word without an accompanying gesture, (even for prepositions and 'ums' and 'ahs') you lose a point. This game can be played in pairs or groups.
- Actors might improvise a scene, or use the chat-show format, interviewing a special guest. All students must participate. A panel of judges should record the score.
- The results will be funny, but the discipline allows for experimentation with gesture and physicality.

Stagecraft
Appreciating drama: Workshop summary

Here is a summary of what was learned in the workshop. Make a record in your logbook.
- Voice and movement are very important when performing melodrama.
- Body language and gesture are actually more important than words when transmitting meaning.

Now, in your logbook, describe the workshop from your point of view. As you do so, answer the following questions.
- How did the exercises help you to explore and understand melodrama?
- Which tasks did you feel most comfortable doing?
- Which tasks did you find more difficult?
- What aspects of melodrama are relevant to performing today? How are they relevant?

The theatres

With the rise of the Industrial Revolution, cities grew rapidly. People left rural life to find work in the factories. Theatres were established in cities, to provide entertainment for the masses.

People from all classes went to the theatre, but they did not mix with one another. Social divisions were reflected in the design of the buildings themselves. Where you sat depended on how much you could afford to pay for your ticket. The cheapest seats were those farthest away from the stage, high up in 'the gods'. Below them was the gallery, which was still a good distance from the stage. The upper classes wore formal dress and sat in the dress circle. They also occupied the stalls, on the floor of the auditorium, as well as boxes, which were located on the dress circle level and sometimes in the proscenium arch itself. Each of these areas had their own entrance and exit points to reinforce the social divisions of the audience.

As the illustration below shows, nineteenth century theatres tended to be large. Some theatres had a capacity of over two thousand people. Coleridge, the famous poet, said of London's major theatres, and which would equally apply to Sydney's Royal Victoria or Melbourne's Theatre Royal, that 'They are too large for acting and too small for a bull-fight'.

Lighting was provided by candles, so it wasn't surprising that theatres burned down on average every couple of years! Gas lighting began to be used in the mid-1850s. Electricity began to be used in theatres from the mid-1880s.

There was no such thing as air conditioning – the air became stale quickly. An evening at the theatre began around 6.30pm and ended around midnight.

Stagecraft

Appreciating drama: The theatres

Sketch a typical nineteenth century theatre in your logbook, marking in the stage, backstage and different social areas of seating. Draw a cutaway side view and a bird's-eye view.

Next, make a brief note of your own explaining how the theatre buildings dictated the form of drama that was produced there. How were the actors influenced by:
- the size of the theatre
- the lighting in the theatre (remembering that there was no way of isolating the stage lighting from the audience lighting)
- the social divisions of the audience?

The plays

The first melodrama was written by a Frenchman, Pixerecourt. An adaptation of his play *Coelina, ou L'enfant du Mystère* was performed at Covent Garden in 1802 under the title *A Tale of Mystery*. The play contained elements which would later be recognised as forming the basis of many melodramas: the Villain – haunted by a secret past; the Heroine – an orphan who later discovers her birthright; and the honest and courageous Hero – destined to get the Heroine in the final scene! Characters were types: good or evil. Music was used to indicate changes of mood and pace, and to heighten emotional impact. Pixerecourt is reputed to have said, 'I write for people who cannot read'.

Melodrama was a far cry from the great literature of Greek drama or Elizabethan drama. It was popular theatre – appealing to the masses.

The plays harked back to the morality plays of medieval drama, which featured the struggle between good and evil. The clarity of the dialogue, the melodramatic style of acting, and the simple plots were easy to follow. Asides, where a character speaks directly to the audience, were often used to keep the audience abreast of the plot, to create tension and to add humour.

A scene from *Lady Audley's Secret* (1863).

Melodrama relied on theatricality. Elaborate stage effects amazed and dazzled the audience. Visual effects such as train crashes, fires, battles, sinking galleons and earthquakes were presented on stage. Often they would dominate the plot and the actors. As the century progressed, sophisticated stage machinery and elaborate decoration led to more and more stunning theatrical effects, which kept the audiences attending the theatre.

Stagecraft

Appreciating and performing drama:
Interpreting a text

Here are two scenes from an authentic script of an English melodrama that was originally performed in 1863. *Lady Audley's Secret* was adapted from a popular novel by Mary Elizabeth Braddon. It was the first melodrama to feature a female villain.

The script contains the original stage directions. First of all, using the set description below, sketch the set of 'SCENE THIRD' in your logbook, marking in the details.

Next, read quickly through the script, and work out who are the virtuous characters and who are the baddies.

Finally, perform a group reading of the script. Cast the characters. During the reading, someone should read the directions aloud. Each reader should try to convey the acting style of their character by using a full vocal range.

As you listen or participate in the reading, try to imagine how it would have been staged in the vast theatre. Where would you have been seated? Imagine the costumes. Imagine the set. Imagine the atmosphere in the auditorium. Afterwards, record any thoughts and ideas you have about the presentation of the play in your logbook.

Lady Audley's Secret

CHARACTERS

Sir Michael Audley	Of Audley Court
Lady Audley	Wife of Sir Michael
Alicia Audley	Daughter to Sir Michael by his first wife
Robert Audley	His nephew
George Talboys	A man of mystery
Luke Marks	A drunken gamekeeper
Phoebe Marks	The lady's maid; cousin to Luke

SCENE THIRD. *A divided scene of two rooms. In R room, a table, chairs, and flight of steps, supposed to lead to a hayloft. At C flat, a door piece with key in it. In L room, a table, chair, and window, showing moonlight perspective.*

Robert and Luke are drinking at table in R room, a candle on table, Luke smoking.

Luke: And that's how the case stands; what I knows I means to let no one else know. You won't get to the bottom of me as easily as I shall get to the bottom of this. *(draining tankard)*

Robert: *(aside)* It will have to be a work of time with this fellow. If I could find a pretext for staying here a few days longer, in some of his drunken moments he might disclose all. I'll not be daunted. No, George Talboys, whether you be alive or dead, I am firm to my purpose to see justice done you.

Luke: What be thee muttering about? This be slow work. Sing us a song.

Robert:	No, no, it's getting late.
Luke:	What o' that? This be my house, the castle, and as every Englishman's house be his castle, in course I be master of the castle, and I say *(rising)* how the castle be going round. *(Music)* My castle be turning into a windmill, I do fancy. *(staggering)* Phoebe, Phoebe! *(calling)* Another tankard of ale!
Robert	*(rising)* No, no, not tonight.
Luke:	I can't sleep without it, it be my nightcap. I think Phoebe has followed the example o' my pipe and gone out. Phoebe. I say! *(calling and trying to light his pipe from candle on table. After several attempts to do so through the following speech of Robert's, he sinks down with his head on table, asleep)*
Robert:	The more I think of it, the more I'm convinced this man is concerned in the disappearance of George Talboys. He is too far gone tonight for me to question him. He scorned my first bribe; my second must be larger. On what other plan can I hit? I'll consider it over a cigar.

(Music. Takes out cigar case and lights cigar. Enter Phoebe and Lady Audley, L room.)

Lady Audley:	Not a word to Robert Audley that I am here.
Phoebe:	Not a word.
Lady Audley:	Send your husband to me.
Phoebe:	I will, my lady, if he's in a fit state.
Lady Audley:	Fit or not, I must see him. I must have no more of his visits to the Hall. Go.
Phoebe:	I don't think you'll be able to make any sense of him. *(exits into R room and shakes Luke)* Luke! Luke!
Robert:	He's too far gone in drink, my dear, to pay any attention to you; and as I don't find him very lively company, I'll go to bed if you please. *(rises)*
Phoebe:	Certainly, Sir. *(lights another candle, which she takes from small table or chimney-piece)* It's not the sort of chamber you have been used to, Sir.
Robert:	It's immaterial to me. An honest man can sleep as sound on straw as on down.
Phoebe:	This is the room, Sir. *(exits R door, followed by Robert)*
Lady Audley:	*(peeping into R room and looking at Luke)* Phoebe was right. I don't think I shall be able to make any sense of him. So Robert Audley sleeps in yonder room – would he slept his last. How am I to arouse this brute without Robert Audley hearing me? I had better wait here until he sleeps. *(re-enter Phoebe, R door, without candle)*
Phoebe:	I wish you could call in the morning, or leave word with me what you would have Luke do.
Lady Audley:	No, this is the only time I have. It is impossible to say where I may be tomorrow. I want you to walk part of the way home with me. Go on the road and I'll overtake you.
Phoebe:	But I'm afraid to leave Luke when he's in drink. He may set the house on fire.

Lady Audley:	*(aside, starting)* The 'house on fire!' A good idea. *(aloud)* Go, go, good Phoebe; if your husband is too far gone to listen to me, I will soon over-take you. Go, go, I say.
Phoebe:	*(aside)* Whatever can she have to say to Luke? *(exit L, Music)*
Lady Audley:	*(looking towards R door)* I wonder if he sleeps. (she peeps in at R door, and speaks through music) All seems quiet. *(locks R door)* He's safe. I have but one terrible agent to aid me, and that is fire.

Music. Lady Audley takes up candle, goes to hayloft, looks into and enters it. The reflection of fire is seen within. She re-enters, and places candle on table, locks the door which parts the room in centre, and exits L door. The fire grows stronger, and Luke wakes up.

Luke:	Why, what is this? Fire. Phoebe, Phoebe! Help, help! *(tries to open door which parts the rooms)* Why, it is fast. Phoebe, Phoebe, I say. Ah! I may escape by this room. *(goes to R door, and tries it)* Why, that be fast too. Oh, mercy, mercy! Help! Help! The fire grows stronger and stronger. Oh, mercy, mercy! Great Heaven. I know I've been a bad and wicked man, but oh save me! Save me, someone! I choke, I choke! I die, I die! Mercy! Help! Mercy!

(Music. Luke staggers and falls, as scene is closed in)

SCENE FOURTH. *The road through Audley Park. In this scene, Alicia runs on to tell Phoebe that Sir Michael Audley has had a fit and is losing speech fast. As Alicia returns to comfort her father, Phoebe is joined by Lady Audley. Phoebe sees the flames coming from her home, but Lady Audley grabs her, stops her from going to help Luke her husband, dragging her in the opposite direction.*

SCENE FIFTH. *The lime tree avenue and well. Moonlight falls on the old well. Phoebe is heard without, calling for help, and is dragged on by Lady Audley, R, Music.*

Lady Audley:	Come, come. To the Hall! To the Hall!
Phoebe:	No, I will not; you mean mischief towards me, I am sure you do.
Lady Audley:	No, girl, no; I am your friend.

(Enter Robert Audley, who, coming between them from L, takes Phoebe from Lady Audley's grasp.)

Robert:	*(to Phoebe)* Away to your husband, girl, and see if there is any help for him.
Phoebe:	Thank you, bless you, Sir. *(exit hastily, L)*
Robert:	*(to Lady Audley)* Now, madam, we will come to a reckoning.
Lady Audley:	*(recoils from him)* Alive!
Robert:	Aye, to punish and expose you. You thought to trap me, to silence me, by dooming me to a dreadful death. But Heaven be praised, I was not sleeping when your wicked hands set fire to the house. No, I live to be your fate, and the avenger of my friend.
Lady Audley:	What will you do? Proceed without evidence? And who are you that dare accuse me? Who are you that oppose yourself to me so constantly? I have wealth, boundless wealth, and I will use it to crush you, to crush you, Robert Audley.

Robert:	How?
Lady Audley:	Thus! *(rushes towards him with poignard. He wrenches it from her hand)*
Robert:	And thus I rob the serpent of its sting!
Lady Audley:	Let me pass.
Robert:	Never! The law shall have its own.
Lady Audley:	And who is to be my accuser? *(Enter Luke, supported by Peasants and Phoebe, L)*
Luke:	I, thank Heaven! I am spared to do an act of justice before I end my guilty life. I accuse that woman of …
Robert:	No! Hold, hold. It will be better not to cast a stain upon my uncle's name. Say nothing, I beg, I entreat of you.
Luke:	Then I will be silent, silent for ever, ever, ever. *(falls back in the arms of the Peasants)*
Lady Audley:	*(aside)* He is dead, and I shall triumph over them all. *(the great bell of the castle is now heard tolling. Enter Alicia from back, followed by servants)*
Alicia:	Robert! Robert! My father is dead. Oh, pity me! Pity and protect me! *(goes to Robert, Music)*
Robert:	Sir Michael dead! Now vengeance, take thy own! Friends, hear me. I accuse that woman of the murder of my friend, George Talboys.
Lady Audley:	How and where?
Luke:	*(revives)* I, I will tell that. She pushed him down that well, *(points to well, all start)* but it will be useless to search there now, for George Talboys is …

(Enter George Talboys, R, Music)

George:	Here! *(Luke falls back dead)*
Omnes:	Alive!
Lady Audley:	*(petrified)* Alive! Alive! You alive!
George:	Back, woman! and thank that man *(points to Luke)* that you have not my death upon your soul. You will be scorned, loathed, and despised by all. The blow you struck me rendered me an invalid for months. I have been silent until today, because I gave my word to that poor, dying wretch. *(points to Luke)* But now I am free, free to tell all. Speak to her, speak to her, Robert, and say I forgive her. *(points to Lady Audley)*
Robert:	*(to Lady Audley)* You hear, woman!
Lady Audley:	*(vacantly)* But I do not heed. I have a rich husband. They told me he was dead, but no, they lied. See, see, he stands there! Your arm, your arm, Sir Michael. We will leave this place. We will travel. Never heed what the world says, I have no husband but you, none, none! It is time to depart. The carriage is waiting. Come, come, come!

George:	What does she mean, Robert?
Robert:	Mean! Do you not see she is mad?
Omnes:	*(retreating from her)* Mad!
Lady Audley:	Aye-aye! *(laughs wildly)* Mad, mad, that is the word. I feel it here, here! *(places her hands on her temples)* Do not touch me, do not come near me. Let me claim your silence, your pity, and let the grave, the cold grave, close over Lady Audley and her Secret.

(Falls, dies. Music. Tableau of sympathy. George Talboys kneels over her)

Curtain

Stagecraft
Making drama: Working with words

In your logbook, write your own version of SCENE FOURTH of *Lady Audley's Secret*. It takes place on the road through Audley Park, and the speaking parts belong to Phoebe, Alicia and Lady Audley.

Work out for yourself what plot development takes place between SCENE THIRD and SCENE FIFTH. The only thing we will tell you is that, during the scene, Alicia brings news of Sir Michael Audley's sickness, and Phoebe sees the flames coming from her home but is prevented from going to help her husband Luke by Lady Audley.

Write as closely as you can in the style of the original.

Stagecraft
Making drama: Working with music

Create you own music soundtrack.

Select either SCENE THIRD or SCENE FIFTH from *Lady Audley's Secret*. In each scene there are four music cues. Select music for each of these cues. This may be done by choosing music from tapes or CDs and re-recording it to accompany a staged reading of your scene. Film music works well. Alternatively, if you are able, you could compose an original soundtrack for the scene.

Look carefully to see what each music cue is doing; whether it is introducing a character or mood, heightening the audience's emotions or providing a dramatic climax to a scene. Avoid using music for comic effect. Try to use it as it would have been used in melodrama, to help the drama.

Navigating Drama

On Your Feet

Melodrama Workshop 2

Warm-up
Students of melodrama must be able to respond physically to different musical cues.

You can stop the music
Play a selection of film music or the recorded music compiled for the Stagecraft exercise on page 101. Walk around the space. When the music stops, everyone must freeze. Anyone seen moving is out. Continue until one person is left.

Responding physically to music
Play the same music. Everyone must move in response to the music, using gestures, movements and facial expressions.

Staging melodrama
The most difficult aspect to overcome when working on scenes that require larger-than-life performance is the tendency to send it up, to make a joke of it. That's the easy way out. Try to find a way of making each line of dialogue work. The object of this task is to explore a dramatic style that has different conventions to realism; it will never feel comfortable.

Working in small groups, choose either SCENE THIRD or SCENE FIFTH from *Lady Audley's Secret*. Each group should complete the following in working towards a staged reading of their scene:

- read through the scene together
- stage the scene for proscenium presentation
- try to incorporate all the stage directions given in the script
- use the music tapes completed for the Stagecraft exercise on page 101
- end your scene with a tableau (SCENE THIRD has none indicated in the script, so make one up)
- spend time constructing a physical characterisation and finding a vocal interpretation appropriate for your character.

Allow about 50 minutes to work through the task. Then present your scene. Afterwards, discuss the effectiveness of the devices of melodrama evident in the scenes.

Stagecraft

Appreciating drama: Workshop summary

Here is a summary of what was learnt in the workshop. Make a record in your logbook.
- In melodrama, actors must respond physically to different musical cues.
- Rehearsal time is important and should not be wasted.
- In tableaux, each actor must stay in character while operating as part of the group.
- In melodrama, an actor isn't asked to *experience* a particular feeling, they are expected to *indicate* the feeling to the audience.

Now, in your logbook, describe the workshop from your point of view. As you do so, answer the following questions.
- Did you encounter any problems staging the scene?
- Did the music help or distract you as a performer?
- How comfortable were you using exaggerated gestures and movements?

The audience

The modern theatre audience is extremely reserved and passive compared to the melodrama audience. In order to fully appreciate the phenomenon of 'attending the drama' in the nineteenth century, it is necessary to understand the vital, energetic role the audience played. The character of melodrama was influenced and developed not by playwrights, theatre managers or critics, but by its audience.

There are recorded instances of actors and theatre managers pleading with an unhappy and noisy audience to let the play continue! The audience had particular expectations concerning the acting style, content, and scenic conventions of melodrama. Any departure from these expectations could result in the failure of a play, or the end of an actor's career! Performances could last up to five hours, and alcohol was freely available. Not only were the actors targets, but members of the audience were often injured or even killed by flying bottles! In order to control such an audience, a dynamic acting style was required.

Explicit sexual references in plays were banned, which is ironic considering that the narrow side-slips of the gallery were often set aside for prostitutes, who would ply their trade during the duller sections of a play. Smoking, drinking, spitting, and even urinating, were ever-present audience pastimes. Toilets were not a feature of theatre design until the twentieth century!

Stagecraft

Appreciating drama: Audience conventions

Make three lists in your logbook.
1 List the conventions of nineteenth century audience behaviour mentioned in the section above.
2 Make a list of the conventions that we observe when we go to the theatre today.
3 Make a list of the conventions we observe when we go to the cinema. How do they differ from our behaviour in theatres, and why?

Australian melodrama

Australian melodrama was a combination of melodramatic intrigue, colonial farce, and topicality. The first Australian melodrama was *The Bushrangers* by Henry Melville, produced in Hobart in 1834. Australian plays developed into the bush spectaculars of the 1870s and ended with *On Our Selection* in 1912, by which time the genre had become almost pure farce.

Australian plays developed their own distinctive flavour.

Characters were bull-voiced bushrangers, noble bushmen, good-humoured diggers, impossibly naive 'new chums', spirited squatters' daughters, faithful Aborigines, and Chinese market gardeners. Titles such as *The Australian Bunyips* and *Coo-ee* indicate the colonial flavour.

Australia's first theatres were based on the English model. Sydney's Royal Victoria Theatre, in which most of the plays by early Australian dramatists were produced, had a seating capacity of 2000. By the 1850s, when Australia's population had reached one million, Melbourne theatres had produced thirty-five new plays by Australian writers, Sydney twelve, and Hobart one. The majority were based on English models, or adhered to an Anglo-Australian pattern: acts one and two take place in England, with characters emigrating en masse in acts three and four, before returning 'home' wealthy in act five.

The best example of Anglo-Australian melodrama is *The Sunny South* by George Darrell, which was first produced at the Opera House, Melbourne in 1883. It includes an attempt to derail a train, and a horse whipping of the Villain by the Australian Heroine.

The Sunny South, Sydney Theatre Company

The Australian Heroine Bubs Berkley is tough, gutsy and full of character, the opposite of the traditional English Heroine. The chief Villain was so odious that on the opening night 'he was several times "called" before the curtain by the audience during the progress of the play that they might hoot and howl at him'. The success of *The Sunny South* consolidated Australian melodrama as a popular form. It was produced twice in London and also in America. The Sydney Theatre Company revived the production in 1980, ninety-seven years after its first production.

Stagecraft
Appreciating and performing drama:
Playreading, *The Sunny South*

Our extract begins towards the end of Act IV of the play. The Australian Heroine, Bubs, has been kidnapped by the Australian Villain, Ben Brewer.

First, read through the script yourself, and work out who are the virtuous characters and who are the baddies.

Now perform a group reading of the script. Cast the characters. Each reader should try to convey the acting style of their character by using a full vocal range.

After the reading, make a note in your logbook identifying the differences and similarities between Australian and English melodrama.

The Sunny South

CHARACTERS

Matt Morley	An Anglo-Australian
Worthy Chester	An English gentleman
Ivo Carne	Of the genus New Chum
Ben Brewer	A representative digger
Eli Grup	A man in charge
Perfidy Pounce	A man of business
Plantagenet Smiffers	An aesthetic gent
Johnny Jinks	A son of the soil
Dick Duggan	A bushranger
Black Steve	His mate
Bank Teller True	A brave example
Black Tracker Jim	A native companion
Narrow Creek Joe	A tintinnabulist
Sergeant Swoop	A hot copper
Monte Jack	A three-card man
Station Master	On the ranges
Engine Driver	Of the special
Bubs Berkley	Bred in the bush
Clarice Chester	Born in the purple
Rebecca Hann	Reared in the kitchen

Diggers, Bushrangers, Policemen, Civilians, Bailiffs

The bushrangers' lair. Enter from hut Dick Duggan, smoking.

Duggan: Not a soul round. Who the devil should there be in such an out of the way place as this? Ha, I'm sick of it. Not a haul to be made without striking the diggings. Plenty of miners with gold and coin there. I'm wasting my time here over that girl – a paltry hundred or two from the lawyer sharp, that's all. I'm full on it and so's the gang. I'll bring her to reason at once. One way or the other tonight shall settle it, and then for the camp and business again.

(he calls. Enter Steve)

Steve: Well, what's up?

Duggan: Bring that girl here at once.

Steve: What, out here?

Duggan: Yes, out here. I want to talk to her – and alone.

Steve: You've had jaw enough, I should think. It's nothink but jaw now – no work and no gold.

Duggan: You got your whack of the sharp's rhino.

Steve: Bah! One good plant and we'd collar ten times as much. Let the girl go.

Duggan: When I like.

Steve: Half a dozen of the cops are hunting her up. There's danger in it, and look here – Blarm me if I stand it any longer!

Duggan: What!

Steve: Put up, you bleeder, or I'll plug yer!

Duggan: I'd blow the top of yer skull off before yer could raise a mauley. Fetch the girl. *(pause)* Go on now.

(Steve exits)

He's right, there is danger – and if 'twarn't for revenge on him and the girl herself I'd let 'em go and be hanged to them both.

(Enter Bubs and Steve)

Steve: Hold on now – none of yer devilments with me.

Duggan: Let the gal go. Let her go, I tell you. What are you frightened at? D'ye think she'll run? Ha, ha. She knows Dick Duggan too well for that. Let her go.

(business)

Go up there on the range and wait till I signal. Be off, d'ye hear. *(to Bubs)* Hold on, you. Stand where you are. Try the bolting dodge, and woman or no woman, I'll drop yer a stiff in yer tracks. You know me.

Bubs: *(slowly)* I do.

Duggan: Ha ha! You do! Ha ha! And that frightens the run out of you.

Bubs: It does not.

Duggan: It does. Why don't you bolt now?

Bubs: Because the blood that's in me won't let me run even from such a cowardly thief as you.

Duggan: What! Curse it, the old pride that thwarted and beat me from the first.

Bubs:	What do you want with me?
Duggan:	What do I want? To tell you once more that you shall never belong to that man – that you shall never be Matt Morley's wife.
Bubs:	(aside) Never, never.
Duggan:	Ha ha, that staggers you. Two years before, when I first asked you to marry me, you rounded on me and he struck me like a dog for daring to speak to you.
Bubs:	He did right – and he'll do it again.
Duggan:	I swore then to be revenged on him and I will. Like a fool I waited, but he hunted me out of the camp.
Bubs:	It served you right.
Duggan:	Did it? Aye, you were in it, you drove me to drink and he forced me to take to the bush and jugged me for the bank job. Between you you've made me what I am.
Bubs:	That's a mean paltry lie.
Duggan:	How?
Bubs:	You were a blackguard from the first – a drunkard, a thief stealing from your mates the gold of the claim!
Duggan:	Damnation! (business)
Bubs:	If you dare!
Steve:	Look out! There's someone crossing the range!
Duggan:	Ah, is there!
Bubs:	Help, there – help!
Duggan:	Stop her! (business)
Bubs:	Help! Help!
Duggan:	Stop your howling or I'll choke you. (enter Dan and Bushrangers) Here Dan, Jim – collar her. (they force Bubs into the hut) Gag her – stop her mouth at any risk. Now quick, Steve – the timber! Ah, that rope may be useful. (Duggan hides. Enter Morley. Steve gets behind tree.)
Morley:	Not a soul in sight. I'll take my oath I heard a cry for help, and the place and the hut tallies with Pounce's description. It's dangerous work alone. I'll go back for the others. (Morley turns to go, and is seized by Steve. Business.)
Duggan:	Move or speak, Morley, and the hammer falls quick. Steve, lash him tight. (Morley is lashed to tree) That'll do. Dan, keep watch inside on the range – see if he's got any pals. Leave him to me! (exit Steve) So I've got you at last. Your life's in my hands. You'll have to beg for it now, you dog. Now, what ye got to say?

Morley:	Nothing, except to tell you that if I stood here free I'd choke the words ere they came from your lying throat.
Duggan:	The same cursed pride, you and the girl! I'll grind it down now and make you both howl for mercy.
Morley:	Never!
Duggan:	We'll see.
	(he calls. Enter Dan)
	Bring that girl here.
	(exit Dan)
	I'm going to have a little picnic with you.
	(business)
	D'ye see the card – the Ace of Hearts? I'm going to fasten it on your left breast (business) and I'm going to drive a hole through two hearts at once.
	(enter Dan and Bubs)
Bubs:	Morley here?
Duggan:	Yes, there he is – dressed up to kill.
Bubs:	Ah!
Duggan:	We're playing a little game of euchre. You drops in and takes a hand and that makes it cut-throat. He leads his ace, and I'm a-going to down it with my right bower.
	(business)
Bubs:	Ah, no, no!
Duggan:	Made you squeal at last, have I? Would you save his life if you could?
Bubs:	Yes. Yes!
Duggan:	You can then. Look here, Matt Morley, that girl will do anything you tell her. Let's cry quits, give me a thousand out o' yer pile, tell that girl to be my wife, we'll clear out of the country, and your skin's safe and sound.
Morley:	No. A thousand times no.
Duggan:	Then die!
	(He fires at Morley, hits him on the shoulder. Bubs screams. Business.)
	Hit on the shoulder only! *(to Bubs)* You've saved his life for a minute by your screeching. Will you save it altogether?
Bubs:	Ah!
Morley:	Don't promise – not even to break it to the murderous hound. Help! Help!
	(Duggan fires. Bubs throws herself in front of Morley)
Duggan:	Ah, I've hit her.
	(Bubs gives cry and falls)
Morley:	Ah, and I'm powerless. Help, there, help!
Bubs:	'Tis nothing – only my right arm.
	(enter Steve from hut with gang)

Steve:	Quick – to cover! There's half a dozen on us, traps and others!
Duggan:	Ah, your arms, boys!
	(gang exit to house)
Steve:	Say, what of this? Shall I stick him?
Bubs:	Ah, Morley!
Duggan:	No. We'll cover him with our rifles and threaten to plug him if they attack us.
Morley:	I cannot aid her – I am powerless. Help! This way quickly, but keep under cover for your lives!
Steve:	That's your last word!
	(business)
Duggan:	You fool – he keeps us safe whilst he's alive – aim straight at his heart and wait till I give the word.
	(shots heard off-stage. Duggan, Steve, Bubs exit to hut)
Brewer:	(off) Come on, mates.
Morley:	Keep to the timber, Ben!
	(enter Brewer, Ivo, Black Tracker Jim and others)
	Don't fire – the girl's there. Charge 'em!
Duggan:	(from hut) Hold on! There's three rifles aimed at that card on Matt Morley's breast. Move a step and three bullets will go through his heart.
Brewer:	What shall we do?
Morley:	Do your duty. Charge the hut.
Duggan:	'Tis certain death to you.
Morley:	Let it come. Yours will follow.
Duggan:	Here, Steve – bring the girl.
Morley:	You fiend, what would you do?
Duggan:	Give 'em another target, ha ha!
Morley:	Quick, boys – rush 'em.
Brewer:	Now, all together!
	(Duggan appears from hut, holding Bubs)
Duggan:	My knife at her throat! Now fire or come on!
Morley:	Ah! The hut is on fire!
Duggan:	What!
Steve:	(inside hut) It's blazing here like fury!
Morley:	Quick – cut me down. Save the girl!
	(shots from hut. Ivo rushes to Morley to cut him down. Ivo is shot, gives cry and staggers back. Brewer catches him. Business.)
	(to Ivo) Are you hit?
Ivo:	Only a scratch on the neck.
Morley:	Free! Come on, follow me.
	(he rushes to door of hut, firing repeatedly)
	Music. Tableau.

Unit assessment

Performing melodrama: The Sunny South

(Six to eight lessons' preparation.)
In groups, prepare the above scene from *The Sunny South* for performance.

- Use appropriate physical gestures and vocal style.
- Stage your scene for a proscenium presentation.
- Include music as part of the performance. Music could be live or pre-recorded but should be used authentically.
- Include a tableau.

In your logbook

- Keep lesson-by-lesson entries, recording your process.
- Afterwards, include a self-assessment evaluating the degree of success in presenting the scene.

Assessment criteria

- Knowledge and understanding of the elements of melodrama
- Use of voice and physicality in presenting character
- Awareness of the conventions of performing on a proscenium stage
- Ability to engage with an audience in a way that is appropriate to the style
- Ability to work as part of an ensemble
- Ability to record and evaluate the process of rehearsal and performance

Assessment feedback sheet

Performing melodrama

	Level of Achievement		
	Developing	Substantial	Excellent

Performance

Use of appropriate physical gestures and vocal style	1	2	3	4	5
Use of proscenium staging	1	2	3	4	5
Ability to engage with an audience in a way that is appropriate to the style	1	2	3	4	5
Ability to work as part of an ensemble	1	2	3	4	5

Logbook

Complete and comprehensive entries reflecting your process	1	2	3	4	5
Post-performance analysis and self-evaluation	1	2	3	4	5

Teacher's comments

_____
_____
_____
_____
_____
_____
_____

Student's comments on their strengths, as well as areas that need more work, thought and attention

_____
_____
_____
_____
_____
_____
_____

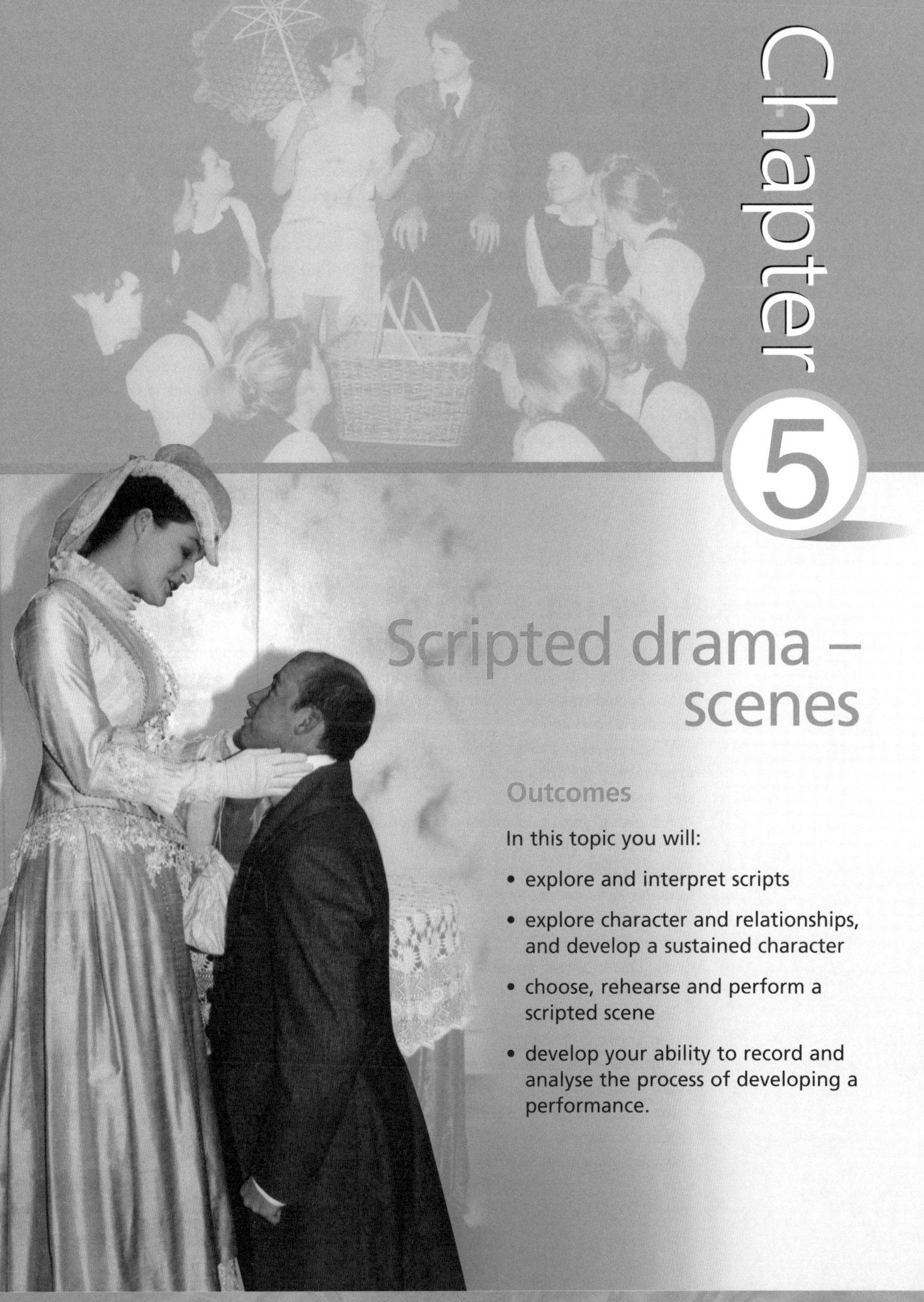

Chapter 5

Scripted drama – scenes

Outcomes

In this topic you will:

- explore and interpret scripts
- explore character and relationships, and develop a sustained character
- choose, rehearse and perform a scripted scene
- develop your ability to record and analyse the process of developing a performance.

What is a script?

A script contains the dialogue spoken by the actors.

The dialogue contains the bare bones of a character, which will be fleshed out by the actor. Scripts are not written, as novels are, to be read. They are written so that performances can be repeated.

Originally, actors carried plays around in their heads, and would travel around performing them whenever there was an opportunity. Later, storylines were written down, and, eventually, dialogue.

Of course there is more to a play than just the dialogue. Yet, no one has yet discovered a way to record the three-dimensional aspects of performance. Although details may be given to establish where the action is set, when the characters enter and exit, and some stage 'business', no attempt is made to detail for the reader what is happening on stage at any time. The only information included is that which helps the reader make sense of the play. Many modern play scripts contain no stage directions at all. The task for you, the actor, is to turn the words into meaningful stage action.

Choosing a script

Preparing scripted scenes from published plays is a valuable experience for drama students. It will acquaint you with the elements of drama.

You should choose your material carefully. The following section will help you recognise a good script.

When you read a script, you begin to discover what is not written down. All you have to help you is the dialogue. You must decide who the others characters are, where they are, what they are doing and why.

A higher degree of imagination is required when reading scripts than with other forms of literature. Because of this, some people find playreading difficult. Even professionals can find it difficult to evaluate a play simply by reading the words; however, there are techniques you can use to develop your skill in reading scripts, and to identify those scripts that will be suitable for your particular needs.

- *Read the character list*, and information about the time and place in which the play is set. This is usually found after the title page.
- *Read the set description* carefully, and make sure you have a picture of the stage firmly in your mind when you begin reading. Imagine it taking place in a theatre space you know.
- Once you have read a few pages and have an initial idea of the characters, actually *cast the characters* in your head. If a character reminds you of someone you know, imagine them as that character. After a few pages you will automatically be seeing that character as you read.
- Make sure you *read the stage directions carefully*. Don't skip over them.

- *Read aloud.* Ideally, reading a play with a group of people is the best way of experiencing it. Dialogue is designed to be heard, not read silently; however, if reading a script alone in your bedroom is your only option, read aloud and give different characters different voices. If your parents want to know who you are talking to, it means you're doing a good job!
- It can also be useful to *make a pencil drawing of the set* and refer to it as you read, to help you understand what is happening on the stage at any point.

A staged playreading.

Stagecraft

Performing drama: Play reading

Read a play aloud in class. Cast the characters. Someone reads the stage directions. Swap roles occasionally to give everyone a chance to read.

Discuss the results. It's often the case that hearing other people's interpretations of a character can broaden your own readings; however, some people don't want to be influenced in this way. What's your opinion? Make an entry in your logbook about this, and note the effectiveness of the play reading techniques listed above.

Play or film script?

It has been estimated that by the time the average person has finished school they have watched more than 19,000 hours of television.

Add thousands of hours for watching movies.

As a result, cinematic techniques are embedded in our subconscious. Television and film scripts tend to present:
- narrow and stereotyped characters
- fragmentary scenes
- repeated shifts in time and place
- incomplete scenes that rely on blackouts for their climaxes.

These characteristics do not work on the stage.

A Doll's House, Ensemble Theatre.

Scenes that provide the best material for the stage actor will:
- have strongly drawn characters
- reveal character through action
- include some character development
- involve a degree of conflict
- be complete in themselves
- build to a definite climax.

Good scripts work on a number of levels. The plot or story is rarely the sole point of interest. Nor does the subject matter of a scene have to be grave or weighty in order for it to be theatrically effective.

Character revealed through dialogue

Identifying who the characters are is the first problem to solve when approaching a script. Some basic details, such as their names, ages and special characteristics, may be given in the cast list, but usually this information is minimal.

As you read the dialogue you will find clues to help you construct an overall impression of each character. This is done by examining the language they use, how they respond to other characters, and how they respond to the situation of the play. A strong script will quickly establish a clear sense of character in a few lines, and will do so indirectly through the dialogue.

Stagecraft

Appreciating drama: Finding a character from the dialogue

You have five minutes in which to write down in your logbook all the information you can discover about Linda and Jenny from this section of dialogue. Afterwards, compare results.

Linda: Have you met Sandra yet?

Jenny: Ahhh yes. She the one with the glass eye?

Linda: That's her. She's amazing. Talk about guts. She'd stand up to a rhinoceros I reckon. And have you run into Margot? She's in for assault. Great chick. Spose if you're that big you're not afraid of anyone. Have you seen the way she eats. Shovels it in.

Jenny: Mm.

Linda: So don't you talk?

Jenny: I talk.

Linda: What's so good about the book?

Jenny: Nothing.

Linda: What is it?

Jenny: Linda, isn't there a rule about when someone's reading or lying down the other one isn't supposed to talk?

Linda:	Yeah, but ... magazines and stuff.
Jenny:	I'm reading.
Linda:	It's a book ... What sort of book?
Jenny:	Science textbook.
Linda:	Science textbook! Yuk. Where did you get that?
Jenny:	Oh, out of the library.
Linda:	Bull. Did that social worker give it to you?
Jenny:	Yes she did.
Linda:	She's a pain in the arse. She should be out saving starving people in the jungle somewhere. She's so good. We call her The Saint. Why did she give it to you? Are you a brain or something?
Jenny:	No, I'm not a brain. She looked up my records and found out I never finished school. I dropped out after I first met Craig and never did the HSC. She thought maybe I could do it while I'm in here.
Linda:	What for?
Jenny:	Good way to spend the time. Better than sitting around doing nothing, she thinks.
Linda:	What do you think?
Jenny:	Maybe.
Linda:	So what are you reading about?
Jenny:	The Mohorovocik discontinuity.
Linda:	Is that a disease?

(from *All Stops Out* by Michael Gow)

Character revealed through action

In studying a character, you first need to look at their outward features. These include such things as the way they move, the way they speak, the language they use, and so on. You will find clues to these features in the script.

Internal characteristics are harder to pin down. In plays, thoughts and feelings can only be revealed through action: what a character does. Look closely at what characters do. It may not be until the end of a scene that a character's motives are revealed.

In every scene each character will have an objective, something they want to achieve. Always look at how a character tries to do this. It may be done through dialogue or through action. Characters who seek to achieve their objective in roundabout ways are far more interesting for an actor than those who try to achieve their aims in a straightforward manner.

The Sport of My Mad Mother, Everyman Theatre.

Character revealed through response to a situation

Some people say that acting is reacting.

Character is often revealed when someone reacts to a situation. Look at the way people cope with difficult situations. It will tell you a great deal about them.

Stagecraft

Appreciating drama: Finding a character through response to a situation

In this scene, the characters realise that they are the last two people on earth. In pairs, as you read it, imagine yourself in the same situation and let it influence your response. After reading the scene, discuss what you have discovered about these two characters and write down your findings in your logbook.

Woman:	Hi.
Man:	Hello.
Woman:	Boy, am I glad to see you.
Man:	Am I glad to see you. I've been looking all over. There's nobody.
Woman:	I thought it was just me.
Man:	Me too.
Woman:	God, are we lucky.
Man:	You're not kidding.
Woman:	You know. I never expected...
Man:	Well, I never expected it either.
Woman:	My horoscope said don't make any plans.
Man:	Well, I guess it's up to us.
Woman:	Huh?
Man:	I guess it's up to us now.
Woman:	What do you mean?
Man:	Well. You being the last woman and me being the last man... we've got to get things started again.
Woman:	Oh, you're right. We've got a lot of work to do. We've got to rebuild, clean up, plant vegetables...
Man:	Yeah, that too. But I was thinking, even more important than that. You being the last woman and me being the last man... We've got to make, ah, things.
Woman:	Huh?
Man:	You know, make little things.
Woman:	Oh, you mean arts and crafts. Stuff like that.
Man:	I was thinking of people.
Woman:	Wait a minute. What kind of a girl do you think I am?

Man:	Now wait a second, you've got me all wrong. I wasn't thinking that.
Woman:	Boy, I've heard some lines before, but this takes the cake.
Man:	No. No. This is not a line. I don't even know your name.
Woman:	You're not going to know my name either.
Man:	Now wait a second.
Woman:	I mean, If you came here looking for a good time, you knocked on the wrong door.
Man:	Now wait a minute. That was the fartherest thing on my mind. I was thinking of this like a public service.
Woman:	What!
Man:	I mean, I'm even willing to marry you.
Woman:	Thanks a lot. Don't do me any favours.
Man:	I'm not doing you any favours. I like you.
Woman:	Oh!
Man:	I mean it. The first time I saw you, I said that's the girl for me.
Woman:	Sure.
Man:	I mean, I bet you're one in a million.
Woman:	Thanks for nothing.
Man:	I mean, I think it's important that we get married.
Woman:	Oh. Well. Oh. Look, I know you're right. I mean after all, if we don't get married, nobody else will. I just feel funny.
Man:	Funny?
Woman:	Funny, we haven't even been formally introduced.
Man:	How do you do?
Woman:	How do you do?
Man:	My name is Alex Halowitz.
Woman:	I'm Mary Elizabeth O'Malley.
Man:	(together) You know, some of my best friends are…
Woman:	(together) You know some of my best friends are…
Woman:	I love you people. I always think you guys are the greatest.
Man:	I love you people. I always watch your parades.
Woman:	Oh, thank you, thank you. I love Seinfeld.
Man:	I think Jimeoin is so funny.
Woman:	He was.
Man:	Well, Mary Elizabeth. Now that we know each other, I guess we should get married.
Woman:	I guess we should. After all, we won't be hurting anyone's feelings.
Man:	That's for sure.
Woman:	It just seems so cut and dried this way.
Man:	What do you mean?
Woman:	Well, I mean, if we met in the old days we could have dated or gone steady, broken up a couple of times.

Man:	If I'd have known you in the olden days, I would have rung up and asked you out.
Woman:	I would have said yes.
Man:	I would have knocked on your door.
Woman:	I'd have opened the door.
Man:	I'd have said, 'Hi there Mary Elizabeth, I've bought you some flowers.'
Woman:	Oh Alex. You shouldn't have done that.
Man:	Do you like them?
Woman:	They're beautiful.
Man:	Then I'd say, 'Hey we're going out tonight. I'm going to take you to the Park Regis. Then to *The Lion King*. Then we'll take a romantic stroll around the harbour.'
Woman:	Then we'll go to the casino and lose some money.
Man:	Yeah, and then we'll go dancing. *(on his knees)* Do you Mary Elizabeth O'Malley, take me, Alex Halowitz to be your lawfully wedded husband?
Woman:	I do. Do you Alex Halowitz, take me, Mary Elizabeth O'Malley to be your lawfully wedded wife?
Man:	I do.
Woman:	Kiss the bride. Let's celebrate.
Man:	Great.
Woman:	Are you hungry?
Man:	I'm starved.
Woman:	I don't have much, just this apple. Have a bite.

(from *The Last Two People on Earth*, author unknown)

On Your Feet

Scenes: Workshop 1

Warm-up

Actors need to develop techniques to focus and relax their mind and body.

Full body relax

Lie on the floor. On your back. Focus your awareness on your breathing. Feel the air travelling in and out of your lungs. Do this for some time.

While lying on the floor, focus your awareness on your body. Begin with the feet. Focus your attention on the soles of your feet. Feel where your heels connect with the floor. Now flex the muscles in the soles of your feet as tightly as you can. Hold for three beats and then relax the muscles. As you do this, imagine any tension being held released into the floor. Slowly, continue this process through the ankles, calves, knees, thighs, hips, chest, shoulders, elbows, wrists, fingers, neck, chin, cheeks, eyes, ears, eyebrows, forehead and scalp. You can do a full body relax at any time, standing up or sitting down. Use it as your personal focusing technique.

On Your Feet (continued)

Voice

You can increase the strength and power of your voice through regular voice exercises.

Standing in a circle, practice these breathing exercises:
- slow, rhythmic breaths in and out with hands on the bottom of your rib cage; you should feel some movement in your hands as your diaphragm expands and contracts
- breathe in, hold for a few beats, them exhale with a hum; continue, feeling the air exhale through your nostrils
- vocalise the vowel sounds, ah, ay, ee, i, o, oo
- add a consonant to the sound, bah, bay, bee, bi, bo, boo
- continue slowly though the alphabet, building up speed
- whisper vowel and consonant sounds with no voice whatsoever.

Articulation is equally important. A strong voice needs clean articulation to be effective on stage.

Impaired speech

Place the tip of your tongue on the bottom of your top row of teeth. Leave it there. Each person says their full name around the circle. The result is comic but a great way of forcing your mouth, tongue and lips to exercise. Each person describes what they had for breakfast with tongues in the impaired speech position.

Tongue twisters

Tongue twisters are also beneficial in making your mouth, tongue and lip muscles more nimble. Master these, repeating each one three times rapidly.
- Red leather, yellow leather.
- Red lorry, yellow lorry.
- Red lolly, yellow lolly.
- Unique New York.
- Good blood, bad blood.
- Mixed biscuits.
- She sells sea shells by the sea shore.
- The sixth sheik's sheep is sick.
- A proper cup of coffee in a proper copper coffee cup.

Hot seat

Improvisation can be a valuable aid for an actor when developing a character.

Hot seat is a group impro exercise. One person sits in a chair in front of the group and answers questions in character.

Students take the roles of Jenny and Linda from *All Stops Out* (Stagecraft exercise on page 116) and Man and Woman from *The Last Two People on Earth* (Stagecraft exercise on page 118). At the start of the session, each pair reads their scene aloud to the class to refresh their memories. Jenny then takes the hot seat. The class will ask Jenny questions, and the student playing Jenny needs to be prepared to improvise her responses as she feels the character would.

Ask probing questions. For example you might ask the Woman:
- Where were you when the explosion happened?
- What happened to your family?
- What did you think when you first saw Alex?

Continue the process with the other characters. End the exercise with a re-reading of both scenes. How different were the final readings? Were the actors able to bring the experience of *Hot seat* into the final reading?

Many students say that completing *Hot seat* gives them the freedom to actually think as the character would in a scene. It allows them to feel more connected to the character and the situation.

Before and after

Here is another improvisation exercise that can be used in developing a character.

Work in pairs. Each pair must devise a short impro using the characters from these two scenes, and create a scene that takes place either before or after the written scene.

On Your Feet (continued)

Spend five to ten minutes developing the following improvisations, then present to the group. Discuss how effective this exercise is in helping to discover the characters, their attitudes, physicalities and personalities.

All Stops Out
Before scene Jenny enters the cell for the first time and meets Linda.
After scene Jenny is studying for her exam. Linda wants to chat.

The Last Two People on Earth
Before scene The Woman is getting ready for a night out. Her mother thinks it's too dangerous to go out at night.
After scene The Man and Woman have their first argument about where to spend their honeymoon.

Stagecraft

Appreciating drama: Workshop summary

Here is a summary of what was learned in the workshop. Make a record in your logbook.
- Actors need to be able to develop techniques to focus and relax their minds and bodies.
- You can increase the strength and power of your voice through regular voice exercises.
- A strong voice needs clear and crisp articulation to be effective on stage.
- Improvisation can be a valuable aid to an actor in developing a character.
- *Hot seat* and *Before and after* are valuable exercises you can use in developing a character's history and discovering who your character is.

Now in your logbook, describe the workshop from your point of view.
- Did the full body relax work in clearing your mind and focusing you?
- How did you respond in the *Hot seat* exercise? Were you beginning to think in character?
- Is it easier to develop an impro when you have a scene to work from? Why?
- What were your strengths and weaknesses in this session?

Character revealed through relationships

Often the relationship between characters will reveal more about who they are than the dialogue or the situation will.

In life we treat people in different ways according to the relationship we have with them. The way you greet your parents or a teacher will be different from the way you greet a friend or classmate.

Good scripts present clear relationships.

Stagecraft

Appreciating drama: Finding a character through relationships

In groups of four read through this scene. Next, in your logbook, list the information revealed in the dialogue: about WHO the characters are, WHERE they are, WHAT they are doing, WHEN they are doing it, and WHY. Finally, based on this information, write a summary of their relationship.

Alistair:	Colin?
Colin:	What?
Alistair:	Have you really ridden a trail bike, or were you pulling my leg?
Colin:	Straight up. Yamaha 250. Twin exhaust, cross-country gear ratios.
Alistair:	Brill.
Colin:	Yeah, it was all right till the brakes failed and I went over the cliff.
Alistair:	You went over a cliff?
Colin:	Yeah. But it's okay, the ocean was underneath, broke my fall.
Alistair:	The Pacific Ocean?
Colin:	Yeah. The surf wasn't too high, only fifteen metres or so.
Alistair:	Brill.
Colin:	Course the sharks were a problem.
Alistair:	Sharks!
Colin:	White pointers. There were a couple of them. Reminded me of the time I had to fight off crocs in the Territory.
Alistair:	Crocodiles?
Colin:	Twenty-footers. I gave them a wrestle for their money but.
Alistair:	Do you know Crocodile Dundee?
Colin:	He's a mate of mine, gave me a few tips. See, a croc's got no brains. You can outsmart 'em. Not like sharks. Only way with sharks is to out-swim them.
Alistair:	You can out-swim sharks?
Colin:	All Australians can. Wouldn't be any of us left if we couldn't. Alistair, don't you ever get bored?
Alistair:	No. Well, a bit. Sometimes.
Colin:	How would you like to help me save Luke's life?
Alistair:	I'm not allowed to give blood!
Colin:	You don't have to give blood. Listen, do you reckon the Queen's doctor would be the best doctor in the world?
Alistair:	Yes, pretty good, specially cos he'd have to do it without looking.
Colin:	Eh?

Navigating Drama

Alistair:	Well, he would, wouldn't he? I mean if the Queen was sick he couldn't just say: 'Take your frock off, Your Majesty, and let me look at your, er... your... you know'. Could he? I mean, not the Queen. Nobody could, could they? He'd have to guess what's wrong. He'd have to be good.
Colin:	Er... yeah. Anyway, I wrote to her and asked her to let me get in touch with him, and she didn't write back.
Alistair:	When did you write to her?
Colin:	Nearly a week ago.
Alistair:	Well, there you are then. It'll be months before she gets round to it.
Colin:	She's a bit slack!

(from *Two Weeks with the Queen*, by Mary Morris, from the novel by Morris Gleitzman)

Group scenes

All the examples used so far have been two-character scenes. Once you have mastered relating to one other person in a scene, you can approach the far more complex problem of playing in multiple-character scenes.

In a three-character scene, relationships are complex. One character may have two different objectives with each of the other characters. In any one exchange, the same dialogue may affect two characters differently.

In the following scene, two friends have arranged to meet a third in a restaurant. They are uneasy about the meeting. The third woman, Monica, has recently suffered a personal tragedy and they are unsure how to treat her. Should they be sympathetic? Should they ignore what has happened and not talk about it?

After Dinner, Chalkdust Theatre.

Stagecraft

Making drama: Conflicting objectives

Prepare two separate readings of the following three scenes.

First reading: In groups of three, allocate parts and then read the scene aloud. Afterwards, discuss your character's chief objective in the piece.

Second reading: Select one objective for your character from the two listed below. Do not tell the others in your group which one you have selected. Now read the scene again and try to achieve your objective.

Dympie:	Objective A	To ally yourself with Paula at every opportunity, to ostracise Monica and prevent her from becoming too friendly with Paula.
	Objective B	To control Monica and keep Paula in line (she is an alcoholic and can be embarrassing in public).
Paula:	Objective A	To ally yourself with Dympie and befriend Monica.
	Objective B	To stand up to Dympie and sympathise with Monica.
Monica:	Objective A	To confide in Dympie and keep Paula at a distance (you suspect she dislikes you).
	Objective B	To befriend Paula and sympathise with Dympie (you believe she is socially inept and has bad breath).

Dympie and Paula are seated at a restaurant table. Monica enters.

Monica:	This is quite nice.
Dympie:	You haven't been here before?
Monica:	No.
Dympie:	She hasn't been here before, Paula, we forgot. This is your first time.
Paula:	Isn't that funny. Seems like you come here with us every week.
Dympie:	Paula and I come here all the time, don't we Paula?
Paula:	Every Friday night.
Dympie:	Well not every Friday night, but often. No, it's all right. Bit of a night out.
Paula:	Beats staying at home.
Monica:	I don't mind staying at home.
Dympie:	Nor do I, Monica, nor do I.
Paula:	But not every Friday night.
Dympie:	No, not every Friday night, Paula. I didn't say every Friday night. But some nights. Then, now and again, it's nice to come out, with the girls – girls night out. Bit of fun. We like it don't we Paula?

Paula:	Yes!
Monica:	I've always been a bit of a homebody.
Paula:	There's the waiter Dymp.
Dympie:	Quickly, Paula, get him!
Paula:	Waiter!
Dympie:	Louder!
Paula:	Waiter!
Dympie:	Waiter!
Paula:	Waiter!
Dympie:	Quickly, Monica!
Monica:	Waiter!
Dympie:	No! Decide on your main.
Monica:	My what?
Dympie:	Your main, Monica. Your main.
Monica:	I thought we were having salads.
Paula:	Waiter! No, we're losing him.
Dympie:	Quickly.
Paula:	No, he's gone.
Monica:	I'm sorry.
Dympie:	See what you've done.
Monica:	I'm sorry.
Dympie:	He knew we weren't ready. He could tell.
Monica:	I'm sorry.
Dympie:	No, it wasn't your fault.
Monica:	I wasn't quick enough.
Dympie:	It was Paula's fault.
Paula:	Mine?
Monica:	I'm sorry.
Dympie:	You're too slow, Paula. You're too slow.
Monica:	I'm sorry, Martin.
Dympie:	No, it's all right, Monica. We weren't quick enough. That's all. Nobody's fault.

Monica is sobbing and choking.

Paula:	Monica?
Dympie:	What's the matter with her Paula?
Paula:	It's all that pent up emotion, Dymp. She's pented it up for ages.
Dympie:	Not now Monica. Now come on. Pull yourself together.
Paula:	Have a little cry, Monica. It's all right.
Dympie:	Is anybody watching?
Paula:	She'll be all right.
Dympie:	Quick, take her to the toilets.
Paula:	She's just having a little cry. Nothing to be ashamed of.

Dympie:	She's going hysterical.
Paula:	Monica... Monica, can you hear me?
Dympie:	Of course she can't hear you. She's hysterical.
Paula:	It's Paula here, Monica. Can you hear me?
Dympie:	Do something, Paula. Slap her, Paula.
Paula:	What?
Dympie:	Slap her!
Paula:	No, I can't.
Dympie:	Slap her!!!
Paula:	No!

Dympie slaps Paula. Monica calms down. Paula is in shock.

Monica:	I think I'm all right now. Thank you.
Paula:	You hit me.
Dympie:	No I didn't.
Paula:	You hit me.
Dympie:	No I didn't.
Paula:	You hit me.
Dympie:	But I didn't mean to.
Monica:	I'm feeling much better now, thank you.
Paula:	You hit me, Dympie.
Dympie:	But I meant to hit her.
Paula:	You've never hit me before.
Dympie:	I know, I'm sorry Paula. I'm sorry.
Monica:	I'm fine now honestly. Just pretend nothing happened. It's just that for a moment I thought Martin was still with me and I panicked. Isn't that silly?
Dympie:	Yes.
Monica:	I was thinking about what I was going to order, when I remembered that I hadn't left anything out for Martin. I thought of him searching through the fridge and not finding a morsel and I panicked because I hadn't done the shopping. I knew that he would be wanting his dinner. I wanted to say something. To tell you that he'd been looking, but I couldn't get it out. It was as if a piece of phlegm had lodged in my throat and my words couldn't pass it. But then I remembered Martin wouldn't be wanting his dinner because Martin's not with me anymore. Martin's dead and the phlegm just slid away.
Dympie:	Are you going to have the veal again Paula?
Monica:	Poor Martin. If only I was a little quicker. To have held him in my arms before he went. But how was I to know? How was I meant to know he was about to die? Men don't have strokes when they're thirty-eight years old. It wasn't my fault. It wasn't my fault was it?
Paula:	Of course not.

Monica:	Have I told you about how Martin died?
Dympie:	Not the details, no.
Monica:	We'd finished our dinner. Martin was in the lounge room watching television and I was in the kitchen doing the washing up. I'd nearly finished the pots when I smelt this most vile smell. So I put the dog outside. But the smell didn't go away. I searched high and low through that kitchen. Martin couldn't stand unidentified smells. Then I realised it was coming from the lounge room. I went in and there was Martin sitting bolt upright in his chair with his nostrils quivering and the most terrible look on his face. He'd be horrified if I told you, but Martin had lost control of his bowels. Something he never normally would have done. 'Martin, is everything all right?', I said. 'No, dear.' And they were his last words. He closed his eyes and slid off the chair. The poor man. He was such a clean person when he was alive. So sad that he had to die in such a shame. Thank God we didn't have any children. And God knows we tried. Still... where would I be now if I had children? Not here, not out on the town having such a good time.

(from *After Dinner*, by Andrew Bovell)

In your second reading how successful were you in achieving your objective? Obviously, some moments would not work, as the objectives were imposed arbitrarily and would have worked against the dialogue.

How different were the two readings because of the conflicting objectives? What did you notice? Can you discuss specific moments in this regard?

Blocking

Blocking is the term used to describe the process of moving actors around on the stage; it is the process of turning a script into stage movement. In this way the written script comes alive.

My Mother Said I Never Should, The Rep.

First you must choose your stage. Which style will you use? Proscenium? Thrust? Traverse? In-the-round? Get to know the advantages and disadvantages of each. Learn about the layout of the stage, its sightlines, where the audience sits, and where the strongest focal points are on the stage.

There are three main types of stage action to consider when blocking a scene.

1. Stage action or movement indicated or implied in the script.
2. Stage action or movement designed to reveal character, inner conflict or subtext.
3. Stage action that serves to make a piece accessible and interesting for the audience.

Stagecraft

Appreciating drama: Stage configurations

Task 1
Here are four different stage configurations. Match each explanation with each illustration.

A *Proscenium*. The proscenium arch is the traditional stage. It is easily identified, as it has a picture frame type arch framing the stage. The actors perform behind the arch, the audience is in front.

B *Thrust*. The thrust stage thrusts into the audience, which sit on three sides of the stage. There are no curtains.

C *Traverse*. A traverse stage has the audience in two sections on either side of the stage.

D *In-the-round*. Theatre-in-the-round is just that. The audience surrounds the stage.

Task 2
'Sightlines' is the term used to describe the best line of sight that the audience has of the stage.

In your logbook, make a copy of these stage configurations. In pairs, discuss which are the optimum sightlines for each different stage. Mark them on your drawing.

On Your Feet

Scenes: Workshop 2

Warm-up
Movement and gesture are as important as voice in translating scripted drama into a performance.

Move as ...
(Approx 30 seconds for each.)
Begin in a standing circle. Move around the space as if you are:
- two years old
- eight years old
- 20 years old
- 50 years old
- 80 years old

- cold
- lost
- tired
- excited
- hungry

- a wild animal
- a dove
- a giraffe
- a mosquito
- a worm

- the colour red
- blue
- yellow
- green
- black.

A group of ...
Seated in a circle, complete these tasks without speaking.
- Become a crowd at a football match.
- Become an audience at an opera.
- Become commuters on a crowded train.
- Become an audience watching a horror film.
- Become mourners at a funeral.

Individual tasks ...
Work in pairs. You are not allowed to use words. Your job is to try to get your partner to:
- sing the national anthem
- laugh like a kookaburra
- stand on one leg and whistle
- cross the room without using their feet
- tap dance in quicksand.

Justifying stage movement
Stage movement isn't natural, but often in scripted drama, it has to appear to be.

You will be given a list of four unconnected movements. Your job is to justify these movements; in other words, to make them connected and comprehensible to an audience. Try to provide logical motivation, and create a sense of place, time and situation through your movement.

Sequence 1: Run in. Stand on one leg. Whistle. Lie on the floor.
Sequence 2: Walk in dragging one leg. Point to the ceiling. Touch your toes. Place a finger in your ear.
Sequence 3: Crawl in. Salute. Sit on a chair. Turn the chair upside down and waltz with it.
Sequence 4: Enter in slow motion. Feel the floor. Hop four times on one leg. Curl up in a foetal position.
Sequence 5: Skip in. Stamp your foot. Wipe your hands on the floor. Wave.

You can make up your own exercises, the more outlandish the better. It is a good warm-up exercise and can produce imaginative and humorous results. All stage movement needs to have a purpose.

Making an entrance
Actors must always know where they are. A sense of place is important.

Discuss how successfully each person creates a sense of place by the way they enter the stage. No dialogue or physical clues should be used. The rest

On Your Feet (continued)

of the group should try to guess what directions have been given.

Enter as if you:
- are walking into MacDonald's
- are entering the principal's office
- are walking into your bedroom
- are arriving at a dance party
- are late for an appointment
- are being pursued
- are walking into a maths class
- are naked
- are suffering from claustrophobia
- are entering a room you have never been in before
- have just been out in the snow
- have just woken up.

Blocking a script

The following script gives no stage directions. Working in groups, block this scene for a proscenium stage.

Colin: Lifejackets! Great. You think we better get ours out? You'd be right. In the water, I mean. Got enough fat on you to keep you warm. I'd be a goner. Whoa, some speed eh? Did you know most plane crashes happen on take-off? Hey, there's Sydney Harbour Bridge. Isn't it beautiful? My brother's in Sydney, in hospital. You reckon they're all lookin' up at us while we're lookin' down? I bet him and all the nurses are lookin' out the hospital window at us. Wave, go on, just in case. I bet he's ropeable, he only got to go in the air ambulance, I'm in a jumbo. Boo sucks Lukey mate! Gor, they don't half feed you a lot. I'm as stuffed as a Christmas turkey. Is that a bit of cancer?

Businessman: I beg your pardon?

Colin: Cancer. It's when the cells start growing too fast inside your body and your whole system can go bung. I've been reading up on it.

Businessman: I know what it is. I just don't particularly want to talk about it.

Colin: Funny that. My folks are the same. Why not?

Businessman: Because it's not a very pleasant topic.

Colin: There's worse topics: Like nuclear war and why sick has bits in it. Only, if you've got it, I'd have it seen to.

Businessman: I haven't got it! I've got indigestion.

Colin: Mum always gets indigestion if she bolts her tucker. You want a go at doing this quiz? Which Prime Minister played cricket for Australia? No? Do you want to colour in this picture of a koala? The crayons are a bit crappy but it was good of the hostie to give it to me.

Captain: G'day Colin. Thought you might like a look at the flight deck.

Colin: Too right.

Businessman: Excuse me Miss, do you have any other seats available?

Colin: Oh, don't worry. I'm going up to the flight deck, so you can have both seats for a while.

(from *Two Weeks with the Queen*, by Mary Morris, from the novel by Morris Gleitzman)

Navigating Drama

Stagecraft

Appreciating drama: Workshop summary

Here is a summary of what was learned in the workshop. Make a record in your logbook.
- Movement and gesture are as important as voice in translating scripted drama into a performance.
- Stage movement isn't natural, but often in scripted drama it has to appear to be.
- All stage movement must be justified.
- Creating a sense of place begins with the actor. If you know where you are, you will create a sense of place for your audience.
- Stage directions in the text need not be followed. Find movements that work for you.
- Move as your character would.
- When approaching blocking, always bear in mind how the audience will see it.

Now, in your logbook, describe the workshop from your point of view.
- How did you respond to the movement directions?
- What are the obstacles with trying to get people to complete tasks when you cannot use words?
- Why does stage movement need to be justified?
- What are the main problems you need to overcome in blocking? How did you solve them?

Working with a script

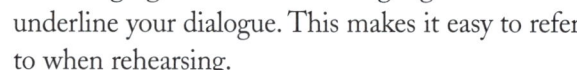

You have been allocated a part in a play.

First, paste your script into an exercise book, one page of script to a double page, leaving the opposite page blank to record staging and notes. Use a highlighter to underline your dialogue. This makes it easy to refer to when rehearsing.

Take your script and a pencil into all rehearsals. Write down the notes that your director gives you. Check through your notes after each rehearsal to make sure you have understood them.

Set aside a regular time each day for learning dialogue.

Neil Armfield directing *The Underpants,* Belvoir St Theatre, Company B.

Working outside the classroom

Many of the tasks required in developing a performance should be done outside the rehearsal room. Good actors are working all the time.

In the early stages of developing a character, observe people, events, places and moods. Mentally take notes. Keep your script with you and jot down thoughts, ideas and observations.

Stagecraft

Making drama: A field trip

Go to a public place, such as a supermarket, mall or sporting event, and observe what is happening. As you watch specific people going about their everyday business, ask yourself a range of questions.
- Why is this person here?
- What sort of home do they have?
- Do they have many friends?
- What are they thinking about?
- What are they going to do next?
- What can I learn about them from the way they dress? And so on.

Collect as many physical examples of the following emotions as you can in your logbook to bring back to class and present either verbally or in mime and movement.
- impatience
- nervousness
- boredom
- irritation
- superiority
- joy
- submission

If you are ever stuck for inspiration when developing a character, look around you.

Researching your character

Often you will need to do research in order to understand:
- a character
- a historical period
- a particular playwright or
- a style of performance.

Restoration drama, for example, features characters in periwigs with white, powdered faces who make grand and extravagant gestures while waving heavily scented handkerchiefs around!

Talk of the Devil, Ensemble Studios.

A little historical research will reveal that this is not merely a theatrical style, but relates to the fact that in the eighteenth century personal hygiene was rather different from today. People did not wash daily, and clothes were laundered infrequently. Consequently, in order not to offend others in social situations, heavily perfumed handkerchiefs were carried and constantly waved around in order to mask any offensive body odours and keep the air around you smelling sweet and fresh. A periwig might conceal lice, and white powder would hide pockmarked facial skin.

With this knowledge, an actor would be able to justify the stylised gestures in a direct way and add depth to the characterisation.

If you need to do some research, begin as soon as you can. Many of the choices and decisions you will make in the development of a performance will depend on your research. Research should be conducted outside rehearsal time.

Character history

All characters have a past.

They were not born five minutes before coming on stage. Constructing a character's history can be a valuable exercise. Find out what you can from the script. Record the information in your paste-down script book and allow it to influence your work in rehearsal.

A word of caution. A character's history is only of value if you can bring it on stage with you. A notebook full of notes about childhood traumas, disappointments, achievements, first loves, is a wasted exercise if it is not used to influence how your character behaves on stage.

Stagecraft
Making drama: Character profile

Use this form when developing a character. Stick it in your logbook.

Name:

Sex: Age:

Physical characteristics:

Family details:

Relationship with other characters:

Personality:

Objectives:

Navigating Drama

*Hard Times,
Ensemble Theatre.*

Using models

Some people develop a character by working from the inside out: analysing their motives and objectives, and only supplying the surface details after they have an understanding of their character's inner life. Others may begin with the external features. These actors work from the outside in. Both approaches are equally valid if the end result is a fully rounded, recognisable and believable character.

Alec Guinness, a fine English actor, said that his first step in creating a stage character was to visit the zoo. Once he received a script, he read it and then went to the zoo to find an animal that he felt was most like the character he was to play. He would observe the chosen animal, its physical movements and social behaviour and use it as the foundation for his stage role.

Some actors say they can only begin to feel comfortable and explore a character when they have found the right shoes. Others use someone they know in life who reminds them of the character they have to portray.

Don't think that you must only use yourself or your own experiences as the basis for developing a character. A good actor is an observer. Be a bowerbird; collect other people's characteristics: their gestures, vocal inflections and laughter, the way they walk and the way they dress.

All these things can be very valuable when finding your way into a stage role. This does not mean that you will simply mimic other people. Through the process of rehearsal, you will combine these physical and vocal adjustments into a character all your own.

Stagecraft

Performing drama: Coping with other actors

Performing is a stressful and demanding activity. People react to stress in different ways.

An actor needs a high degree of sensitivity. In your logbook, note these informal rules that should be observed in order to keep a productive working relationship with your fellow actors.

- Never be late.
- Warm-up as a group.
- Always be aware of other people's feelings.
- Help each other out of trouble on stage.
- Never criticise another actor's performance.
- Don't lay blame; look for a solution.

- If a problem occurs during a performance, have a post-mortem to make sure that the problem doesn't happen again.
- Don't touch another actor's props or costumes.
- Leave personal dramas out of the rehearsal room.
- Be disciplined backstage; move carefully, speak in whispers.
- Mark stand-bys in your script – well before entry cues – so you will never miss an entrance.
- Your stage manager is God; don't argue, obey.
- Take responsibility for your own props and costumes; put them away carefully after each performance; lost props and costumes are your problem, no one else's.

Unit assessment

Performing drama: Performing scripted drama

(Four to six lessons' preparation.)

In groups, prepare *The Last Two People on Earth* or the scene from *After Dinner* or a scene approved by your teacher for performance.

- Develop a clear character.
- Choreograph your blocking.
- Learn the dialogue.

In your logbook

- Keep a lesson-by-lesson account of your process.
- Include a character profile and character history.
- Include an annotated script containing blocking and any other relevant information.
- Complete a post-performance self-evaluation discussing the strengths of the project from your point of view.

Assessment criteria

- An understanding of the elements of drama
- Use of voice and physicality in presenting character
- Ability to engage with an audience
- Ability to work as part of an ensemble
- Ability to record the process of rehearsal and performance

Assessment feedback sheet

Performing scripted drama

	Level of Achievement		
	Developing	Substantial	Excellent

Performance

Use of voice and physicality in creating a character	1	2	3	4	5
Appropriate and effective staging	1	2	3	4	5
Audience engagement	1	2	3	4	5
Ability to work as part of an ensemble	1	2	3	4	5

Logbook

Completes entries for each session	1	2	3	4	5
Post-performance self-evaluation	1	2	3	4	5

Teacher's comments

_____
_____
_____
_____
_____
_____
_____

Student's comments on their strengths, as well as areas that need more work, thought and attention

_____
_____
_____
_____
_____
_____
_____
_____

Chapter 6

Scripted drama – monologues

Outcomes

In this topic you will:

- explore the theatrical possibilities of solo performance
- demonstrates skills and knowledge of the dramatic monologue
- understand the dynamics of the actor–audience relationship
- record the process of rehearsal and performance.

Navigating Drama

Choosing a monologue

A monologue means that one person is alone, on stage, speaking aloud.

The script for a monologue may be written by a playwright especially for that purpose. It is more likely, however, that the material for a monologue will be taken from a full-length published playscript.

So the first decision is how to choose material from a scripted play that will make an effective monologue. Look at the following:

Lt Col Graham: War Office, Whitehall, London. 10th April, 1916. Mrs Sarah Simpson. Madam, I have it in command from His Majesty the King, to inform you as next-of-kin of the late Private John Simpson, No. 202, of the Australian Army Medical Corps, that this Private was mentioned in a Despatch from General Sir Ian Hamilton, dated 22nd of September 1915, and published in the Supplement of the 'London Gazette' dated 5th November 1915 for gallant and distinguished service in the field. I am to express to you the King's high appreciation of these services and to add that His Majesty trusts that these public acknowledgements may be of some consolation in your bereavement.

(from *Simpson, J. 202,* by Richard Beynon)

Although this passage may be dramatically effective for an audience watching a production of the play, there is little to be gained from presenting it as a monologue. It doesn't stand alone as a gripping piece of theatre. It merely imparts information. The language is formal, containing several dates and names. An audience would need to know more about Simpson and his history in order to become involved in the piece.

There is little dramatic content in this monologue.

Now look at this script:

(Cemetery. Cherie stands by a grave.)

Cherie: It was my fault. If we stuck together like we said, you and me and Leanne, you wouldn't be here. But I lost youse all. Now I've lost you. And no one knows how. You should hear the rumours. Someone seen a black Torana with Victorian number plates. It was a stranger in a Megadeth T-shirt, it was a maddie from the hospital, even your stepdad. All these ideas about who did it, like it was a TV show. It is a TV show. Every night on the news. I want to yell out, this is not a body, this is Tracy you're talking about. Someone who was here last week, going to netball, working at the Pizza Hut, getting the ferry, hanging out. You were alive. Now you're dead. But I know you can hear me. I can hear you. Your song. Times we danced to that, you and me and Shana singing dirty words, remember? Mum hearing and throwing a mental ... I shouldn't laugh, should I? Not here. But all I can think of is the other words. You were wearing my earrings. You looked so great. And some guy took you off and did those things to you. Wish I knew who. You know, Trace. Nobody else does. If I knew, but, I'd go and kill him. I'd smash his head in. I'd make him die slowly for what he did to you.

(from *Blackrock,* by Nick Enright)

This passage is part of a full-length play. Cherie's character comes through with some force, and her relationship with Tracey is clearly defined, so an actor has plenty to work with.

A monologue should stand on its own as a performance piece and not require a program note in order to make sense to an audience and be effective.

Stagecraft

Appreciating drama: Scripts suitable for monologues

Examine these two passages of dialogue. They have been taken from play scripts. Which of them do you think might make an effective monologue, and why? Write notes in your logbook discussing both excerpts. Indicate the limitations of any piece you consider to be unsuitable.

Passage 1

Vickie: Tom came round to my parents' house and told us. It was about half past two in the morning. His face was white. I realised something was wrong. 'It's David', he said. Apparently David had got in with a bad crowd. They'd broken into a chemist's shop and taken some money. They thought they'd got away with it but the security cameras had some pictures of him and the police went round to his mother's flat. His mum rang him up: She was ropeable. David loved his mum. He was very depressed. That night he went drinking with some friends but he left them about eleven. He must have gone straight to the bridge. The police found him just after midnight. His neck was broken.

(from *Cornerstone*, by Stephen Holt)

Passage 2

Colin Brunner: All right
now listen up
and that includes you, Dowland!
I've seen tough guys before
my oath I have
I've seen customers who thought they were
Bruce Willis and Arnie Schwarzenegger
rolled into one.
I've seen guys who thought they were King Kong!
So don't give me that
butter-wouldn't-melt-in-my-mouth look
don't give me that
I-don't-know-what-you're-talking-about look
because you don't fool anyone
you couldn't even fool your own blind grandmother!
I'm talking
about last night's little episode –
what are you looking at Dowland
I'll give you something to look at in a minute! –
last night's little episode
gentlemen

which involved five members of this team
stealing a car
and taking it
on one little joy-ride
too many.

(from *The Fifth Quarter*, by Don Whittager)

When you have discussed your findings, you might like to refer to the *Notes* on page 157.

Conflict

All drama is based on conflict.

In a play where there are several characters on stage, conflict is usually revealed through dialogue. It can also be revealed through the action, the plot and the ideas in the play.

How can you solve the problem of conveying conflict in a monologue when there are no other characters on stage?

Firstly, it is possible to show a character in conflict with another person who is not present:

Sal: *(she is reading a newspaper, then begins to tear it up)* Who do you think you are, George McCabe? Are you happy now? Are you satisfied? Everyone loves George McCabe. Isn't that a joke! Everyone knows you but your own daughter, your own Sal. *(pause)* You were never home, never there, were you? Remember the time I had my appendix out? Just turned eight. The pains came only a few days after my birthday. In Broome, they said. 'Daddy's singing in Western Australia', the nurse said. 'We're all very proud of him.' Proud! I wanted you with me! I wanted to feel your arms around me and hear you saying that it would be all right. *(pause)* It never was all right, was it Daddy? When I failed my exams you never wrote me. Were you ashamed of me? Was that it?

(from *George McCabe*, by Colleen Reagan)

Secondly, a character may also be in conflict with themselves. This inner conflict can create an effective stage monologue:

Will: I should have told them. Shouldn't I? It was such an easy thing. Not difficult. Not really difficult. So why did I keep quiet? Was it cowardice? It wasn't as if I had anything to hide. I saw the whole thing. I saw the ditch-digger and the car ahead of me and I knew what was going to happen. I

Road,
Ensemble Theatre.

watched it all in slow motion. It was horrible. The Corolla hit the digger, never saw it, spun into the traffic and was slammed into by a lady in a blue Mazda. I slowed down as I came to the wreckage. I saw the man on the road. The door had flown open and he was lying on the road. *(pause)* I drove on. My God, why didn't I stop? I don't know. I panicked and drove on!

(from *Close Shave*, by Mike O'Neill)

Thirdly, a more subtle sort of conflict can be created between the tone of the speech and the expectations of the audience. For example, an audience might be amused by a section of lighthearted dialogue, while all the time realising that it is leading to a tragic conclusion:

Ali: I dyed my hair blonde. Learnt to walk with a wiggle. Practised in front of a mirror. In my bedroom. Gives you a real sore neck. Well it did until I fell over the laundry basket. Managed to disguise the limp. Saturday came and I turned it on. Little black dress, you know. Mark called at eight. *(pause)* Said he was in films, casting agent. Knew all the names, Beresford, Campion, Noyce, Buttonshaw. 'Buttonshaw', I said, 'Who's he?'. 'Never heard of 'im, darl?', says Mark, always the gentleman. 'I'll introduce yer.' *(pause)* Didn't get into films straight away. Began waiting tables at the Rialto. Good job although it got cold in winter. It was topless, see. Yeah. One of the rules. I got by though. Lucky to have a job really. Many of my friends were out of work. Didn't need a character reference either! *(pause)* I'm in films now. *(pause)* It's not like I imagined. *(pause)* I make about two a week.

(from *Marilyn, Where Are You Now?*, by Kirsten Rose)

When selecting material for a monologue, look for the conflict. Scenes that have several levels of conflict at work make for the best drama, and potentially, the best monologues.

Stagecraft

Appreciating drama: Identifying conflict

The following two extracts contain different kinds of conflict. Write notes in your logbook discussing both excerpts, identifying the type of conflict in each case.

Passage 1

Danny: Ridiculous, ... Yes, that's what it is: ... ridiculous! These are supposed to be peace times ... These are supposed to be civilised people ... We're supposed to be the savages ... Yet none of my people have been the savages ..., the barbarians that your people are! ... You white people have declared war on my people, but you're not doing it in the open ... like men ... Oh, no ... It's a sneaky snivelling war ... a war of worms that slither around and poison poor gentle people whose only wrong was that they were on the land that the worms needed. *(Danny pulls some papers from his shirt)* Here ... Read ... They fell out of an old cupboard in the old stores at the hospital, when we were cleaning up ... Here ... a report of poisoned bodies of Aboriginal people ... Traces of strychnine found in flour ... found in water holes ... no charges laid ... *(Danny cries out)* If your mob want war ... they'll get it ...

(from *The Keepers*, by Bob Maza)

Passage 2

Sloane: It's like this see. One day I leave the Home. Stroll along. Sky blue. Fresh air. They'd found me a likeable permanent situation. Canteen facilities. Fortnight's paid holiday. Overtime? Time and a half after midnight. A staff dance each year. What more could one wish to devote one's life to? I certainly loved that place. The air round Twickenham was like wine. Then one day I take a trip to the old man's grave. *Hic jacets* in profusion. Ashes to Ashes. Alas the fleeting. The sun was declining. A few press-ups on a tomb belonging to a family name of Cavanagh, and I left the graveyard. I thumbs a lift from a geyser who promises me a bed. Gives me a bath. And a meal. Very friendly. All you could wish he was, a photographer. He shows me one or two experimental studies. An experience for the retina and no mistake. He wanted to photo me. For certain interesting features I had that he wanted the exclusive right of preserving. You know how it is. I didn't like to refuse. No harm in it I suppose. But then I got to thinking ... I knew a kid once called MacBride that happened to. Oh, yes, ... so when I gets to think of this I decide I got to do something about it. And I gets up in the middle of the night looking for the film see. He has a lot of expensive equipment about in his studio see. Well it appears that he gets the wrong idea. Runs in. Gives a shout. And the long and the short of it is I loses my head which is a thing I never ought to a done with the worry of them photos an all. And I hits him. I hits him. *(pause)* He must have had a weak heart. Something like that I should imagine. Definitely should have seen his doctor before that. I wasn't to know, was I? I'm not to blame.

(from *The Entertaining Mr Sloane*, by Joe Orton)

When you have discussed your findings, you might like to refer to the *Notes* on page 157.

Characterisation

When choosing a monologue look for a clearly drawn character.

This does not mean someone about whom you know a lot of facts, such as name, physical description, favourite foods, and so on.

Clearly drawn characters are those you feel you *know well* after reading the script. They are three-dimensional. They are real.

Their characters are revealed through the language they use, the actions they take, the choices they make, and the objectives they work towards in the play.

Our Lady of Sligo, Belvoir St Theatre, Company B.

Stagecraft

Appreciating drama: Clearly drawn characters

Read these two pieces of dialogue. Which one do you think exhibits the most clearly drawn character? Make notes in your logbook on both scripts, giving reasons for your choice.

Passage 1

Dave: My father was a secondary school teacher who taught classics. He believed in scholarship, accuracy, integrity. The walls of our house were covered with maps and charts, reproductions of great paintings. For a long time, I remember, we had in the dining room a 'Wines of France' map on the wall, and in the kitchen a huge one of the South Island with trails of dots in red ink indicating the tramps he'd done as a young man. He tried to instill his love of tramping into us, forcing us over mountain passes, pointing out far-off peaks or native flora while we straggled behind as far as possible, a sulking mass of indifference. His greatest ambition was to take us all to Europe and to retrace some of Hannibal's route over the Alps and to follow the trail of Chaucer's pilgrims to Canterbury. Of course we never made it, thank God. Mealtimes in our house weren't occasions for conversations; rather they were opportunities for him to lecture us on the Greeks' use of herbal medicines, or the decline of the Roman Empire through their neglect of having a

Navigating Drama

numeral for zero. On his retirement from the school, he gave a predictable speech deploring the decline of interest in the classics; found, with all the time he needed at last, that his own interest had declined and died.

(from *The State of the Play*, by Roger Hall)

Passage 2

Aggie: I always hoped I'd never have to leave Narrabri. Every person I knew in the world lived there. But Dan had to go where the work was. We couldn't sit and starve. So we came to Sydney and went into that residential. A pokey little room in Surry Hills with the use of a kitchen! Oh, it was awful. The kids weren't allowed to do this and you weren't allowed to go there. We'd all been used to running free and now we were harnessed. And lonely. Dan seemed to be away from earliest morning until late at night either looking for a job or labouring at one. Like I said, I didn't know a soul and not a soul seemed to want to know me. I remember one day I couldn't bear it any more. I decided to go for a long walk. Bernard was the eldest. I left him in charge of the others and I made up my mind to go straight and not turn any corners so that there wouldn't be a chance of my getting lost. Well, I suppose I got gawking at the people in cabs and the things in shop windows and unbeknown to myself I wandered into Oxford Street. Suddenly, I didn't have any idea of where I was. It was as if I'd been picked up and dumped down in some other country. I was sure I'd never see Dan and the kids again. I was too frightened to ask the people passing by where I was. All the men looked like brutes and the women had rouge on their cheeks. Finally, I came to the Sacred Heart and I went inside. But the only sign of a priest was a light over a confessional. So I went in there. The poor fella got such a shock. After I'd blessed myself and said that bit about, 'Forgive me, Father, for I have sinned', I burst into tears and sobbed: 'Can you tell me the way back to Crown Street?'. Oh, but he was very nice about it. He came right out of the box and called to one of the boys in the school yard and got him to take me all the way home to my door. Of course it was a long time after that before I went out by myself again.

(from *A Hard God*, by Peter Kenna)

When you have discussed your findings, you might like to refer to the *Notes* on page 157.

Content

Your monologue must have something to say.

Without content, drama cannot be effective.

'Content' refers to the meaning of a scene and the themes it is exploring. No amount of dazzling costuming, breathtaking settings, or whizz-bang stage mechanics can compensate for a lack of content. Although it is possible to start at any point in developing a monologue, the question 'What am I saying to an audience?' should be the guiding principle throughout the process.

If your monologue is taken from a full-length play, read the entire play. Use it to help you understand the content of your piece.

If you understand the meaning of your monologue, you will find learning the dialogue much easier. An understanding of the text will also give you ideas about how to stage your monologue.

Talking Heads,
Ensemble Theatre.

Performing a monologue

In acting terms you never talk to yourself on stage.

A monologue might be better described as a two-scene. So who is the character on stage talking to? The audience?

Of course the audience is meant to be listening and absorbing what you are doing. A major element that makes a monologue 'drama', rather than just a reading, lecture or speech, is the involvement of the audience. The actor must always ask: 'What do I want the audience to think, feel, know, fear or suspect?'.

But when asked: 'Who am I talking to in my monologue?', the answer cannot be 'the audience!'. The actor may be addressing the audience, but who is their character speaking to?

The answer will depend on the piece. Who is the preacher speaking to in the following extract?

Preacher: Brothers and sisters. We gather here today to mourn the passing of our dear departed brother Eli. Eli was a man known to us all; we know of his failures and his victories on his journey through life, and I know that God will be aware of them also. Because God is compassionate and because God cares. We know that as Eli steps over the threshold into His presence, he will be met with sympathy and understanding. White people do not have a monopoly on heaven, because there in God's house all men are equal. If Eli Wallitch suffered inequality and injustices in his life, he will – believe me! Believe me! – find equality and justice on the big reserve on high.

(from *Barungin,* by Jack Davis)

The preacher is speaking to a congregation gathered at a funeral service. An imaginative actor would not have much difficulty in relating to the audience as if they were a congregation gathered in a church. If you were playing the preacher, you would have complete freedom to address specific individuals, maintain eye contact with them and speak to all members of the audience.

However, in many monologues it will not be as easy to determine who you are speaking to. In the next piece of dialogue, it is clear who the wife is talking about, but who is she talking to?

Wife: What's happened to him this evening? Must be a world crisis if he's actually forgotten to come padding out to carry his tray. Perhaps he's finally given it up. Thank heavens for that. Forever running in and out with his tray. Why doesn't he behave like a man? I'd like to know what he's done with the whistle off that kettle. Where is he then? ... Go on, go on stir away. I've had three cups by the time he's finished stirring his first. I wouldn't mind if he'd remembered to put sugar in it. And if he expects me to sugar it for him, just so he can complain it's too sweet ... I'm so tired.

(from 'Countdown' from *Mixed Doubles*, by Alan Ayckbourn)

The wife appears to be talking to herself, or thinking aloud. Although this is a theatrical convention that most audiences will accept, in real life people do not usually talk to themselves.

How would you, as an actor, justify a character voicing their thoughts in this way?

The magic 'as if'

Once you have determined why a character is talking to themselves, you must explore how to do it. A useful technique for dealing with this acting problem is the magic 'as if'.

Stagecraft

Making drama: Using the magic 'as if'

The following exercise suggests a practical method of dealing with the problem of talking to someone who is not there, using the example from Ayckbourn's script above.

1. One person sits on the stage, in front of the group, and reads through the part of the wife.
2. Next, place two chairs either side of the wife. Two students sit in the chairs. One person takes the part of the husband, and the other becomes a close friend to whom the 'thoughts' are spoken. Read through the dialogue a second time, with the wife relating to each actor where appropriate. Compare this reading with the first read-through.
3. Remove the third chair and place the friend among the audience. Complete a third reading with the wife addressing the 'thoughts' to the friend. Discuss the results.
4. Repeat the exercise with the wife speaking to the whole audience 'as if' they were the friend, or a group of friends.

Discuss the differences between the first and last readings.

By specifying who you are talking to, and experimenting with ways of making it work for an audience, your monologue will be more involving. Your character will appear more natural and less stagey.

Specify exactly who you are talking to. Don't just give the person a name, but decide on their physical appearance, their character traits, and their relationships. Create detail. The end result will be animated, contain light and shade, and be more believable for the audience.

Specifying who your character is talking to, and utilising an appropriate 'as if', will help you construct a clear characterisation, justify the performance style, establish a workable relationship with the audience, and present a range of staging ideas for experimentation.

On Your Feet

Monologue: Workshop 1

Warm-up

In performance, you must use the full range of vocal register: upper, middle and lower.

Moving the voice

- Start with slow, rhythmic breaths in and out with hands on the bottom of your rib cage to feel the diaphragm moving.
- Vocalise a gentle hum as you exhale; repeat several times; be aware of the air moving in and out.
- In your middle register, vocalise: 'memory, memory, memory'; repeat three times
- Repeat in upper register.
- Repeat in lower register.
- Now, move your voice from the lower, through to the middle and into the upper register with the following:
  – 'my mother minds my money'
  – 'ming, mang, mong, mung'.
- Repeat each three times in each register.
- Reverse: go from upper to middle to lower register; repeat three times.
- Repeat ten times, each time placing your voice a little lower and higher with each repetition.

Concentration

In performance, you need to have high levels of concentration and observation.

The mirror

In pairs, sit on the floor opposite your partner. One student performs the mirror image of the other. In slow motion, take turns leading with arm movements and facial gestures. Maintain eye contact. Use your peripheral vision to move in unison. An observer should be unable to pick who is leading. On a given cue, switch leaders.

Bank, river, boat

Designate these three positions:
- BOAT: everyone clumped in the middle of the space
- BANK: the extreme sides of the space
- RIVER: in between.

Students move to each position when called, and then freeze. No running. No speaking. The last person to get there (or move) each time is out. Continue until one person wins.

Using the magic 'as if'

By specifying who you are talking to, and experimenting with ways of making it work for an audience, your monologue will be more involving. Your character will appear more natural and less stagey.

On Your Feet (continued)

In pairs, read through both of the following extracts and complete each task below.

Passage 1

Annamae: If I had one wish in my life, why, I'd like to live in McDonald's. Right there in the restaurant. 'Stead of this old place. I'll come up to the brow of the hill, bowed down with my troubles, hurtin' under my load and I'll see that yellow horseshoe, sort of like part of a rainbow, and it gives my old spirit a lift. Lord, I can sit in a McDonald's all day. I've done it too. Walked the seven miles with the sun just on its way, and then sat on the kerb till five minutes of seven. First one there and the last to leave. Just like some old French-fry they forgot. I like the young people workin' there. Like a team of fine young horses when I was growin' up. All smilin'. Tell you what I really like though is the plastic. God gave us plastic so there wouldn't be no stains on his world. See, in the human world of the earth it all gets scratched, stained, tore up, faded down. Loses its shine. All of it does. In time. Well, God, he gave us the idea of plastic so we'd know what the everlasting really was. See, if there's plastic then there's surely eternity. It's God's hint.

('French Fries' from *Talking With*, by Jane Martin)

Passage 2

Jimmy: You should have caught me auditioning for a TV commercial last week. Now get this scene: nine men and three women glued together behind this long conference table starin' at me like they're producing 'War and Peace meets Ben Hur!' instead of a one minute commercial for some new soft drink 'Squirt/Splash/Squat/Snatch', something momentous like that. Catch the director: 'Mr Zoole – Zoole, is that right – ah – your real name?'. No – like I changed it for the stage, right? 'Yes it's my real name'. 'Mr Zoole, here's our scene: You dive into a pool, swim the length, jump out, shake off the water, and our spokeswoman hands you the drink. You take a sip and say, 'Wow, that's the most refreshing – what is it? Only one line, but it's important. Think you can handle that?'. Well, I don't know. I've only been in the business twenty years. Maybe I should start out with something simple like: 'Da-da, goo-goo, kah-kah!' 'Yes, I think I can handle that.' 'Okay Mr Zoole, dive in!' Dive in! He actually wants me to dive in. And I swim the length of the conference table. Up, out, shake it off. And I'm just reaching up for this non-existent can when the director says, 'Wait a minute, Mr Zoole, you didn't look as if you were enjoying the swim.' Oh, Christ, how I wanted to say: 'No, you see, there was a little speck of shit in the pool – you!' But, see – you want the job. You want it so badly that – glamorous! I got a million of 'em. I got a humiliation a minute. I got a humiliation a lifetime. I'm so tired of being charming and nice to everyone.

(from *PS Your Cat is Dead*, by James Kirkwood)

1. Each pair should make their own choices about who is being spoken to, and experiment with the magic 'as if' and explore the possibilities. There are no right answers. Different individuals will make decisions based on their interpretation of the dialogue.
2. After each pair has made decisions about who the character is talking to, they should work on developing a staged reading of their piece. Share the roles of director and performer.

Many of the monologues previously included in this chapter would also be suitable for this exercise. These comprise those spoken by Cherie, Jacques Roux, Sal, Will, Ali, Danny, Sloane, Dave and Aggie.

Present the scenes and evaluate their effectiveness.

Stagecraft

Appreciating drama: Workshop summary

Here is a summary of what was learned in the workshop. Make a record in your logbook.
- Use your full range of vocal register to make your piece theatrically effective.
- In performance, you need to have high levels of concentration and observation.
- Determining who your character is speaking to can help with understanding and performing your monologue.
- By specifying who you are talking to, and experimenting with ways of making it work for an audience, your monologue will be more involving. Your character will appear more natural and less stagey.

Now describe the workshop from your point of view.
- Give an honest evaluation of your vocal skills.
- How successful were you at the concentration and observation exercises?
- How would you rate your powers of concentration and observation?
- Describe how you utilised the magic 'as if'.
- How did the other students react to the tasks?

Using references

The actor Spencer Tracey was highly regarded for his relaxed and detailed style of acting. When asked how he went about his work, he is reputed to have said that acting involved just two things: 'listening, and meaning what you say. And if you think that's easy, try it!'

'Using references' is a technique to help you 'mean what you say'.

If you are talking about people, events or places that you have no experience of, use an 'as if'. In your mind, substitute a person, event or place that you do know. If you use these personal references, the result will be more believable.

Without any preparation, read the following lines aloud:

> *She had an interesting face. She wasn't what you'd call beautiful, but she stood out in a crowd. It's hard to describe what it was. Her eyes would smile at you as she spoke. And her laugh. It made you laugh along with her.*

Now, imagine someone you know and read the lines as if you were talking about that particular person.

What differences did you notice between the two readings? If you perfect this technique, you will be able to create a feeling of spontaneity for the audience, and your character will be more believable.

In performance, 'references' can suddenly make a monologue come alive. Over time, references may become stale. If this happens, choose new ones.

Single Spies, Ensemble Theatre.

Navigating Drama

On Your Feet

Monologue: Workshop 2

Warm-up

Vocal and physical warm-up exercises can have a beneficial effect on developing your performance skills. Warming up your mind is equally important.

Movie, Song, Book: In a circle

First person starts by saying the name of a movie. Next person has to say a movie, book or song beginning with the last letter of the title given by Person 1. Continue around the circle. After one round, introduce speed, and penalties. If you hesitate, pause or dry, you're out.

I went shopping

This child's game is great for exercising your memory. Playing it regularly makes you better at learning dialogue. Person 1 begins by saying, 'I went shopping and bought.' (mention an item); Person 2 repeats the exact phrase and adds their own item. Continue around the circle. If any player forgets an item, mime the item for them.

Alphabet without the vowels

Go through the alphabet as fast as possible, a letter at a time around the circle, omitting the vowels. (This exercise works best if one person stands in the middle of the circle and orchestrates each response by clicking or pointing.) They can increase the tempo, and change between random or sequenced responses. If you accidentally supply a vowel, you're out.

Distractions

Begin with two students. Person 1 has to count backwards from 100. Person 2 must distract them. They can do anything they like except touch them. Person 1 must keep eye contact at all times. Hesitate, laugh or make a mistake in the count, you're out. Appoint a student to be the number judge.

Using references

Using references is a technique to help you to mean what you say on stage.

You should have no difficulty in using references for the following speech, even if you don't agree with Sam's opinion of school. Look over the speech and choose references for everything Sam is discussing. All members of the group should prepare the exercise. Two to three students then volunteer to perform the piece. Do personal references help to make each performance different?

Sam: Remember when you first said you hate school. I despise school. It just gets in the way. That book I was reading on the beach that day, that had nothing to do with school. It was a book by someone I read about in a book about the novel we're supposed to study. I hate the stuff we're supposed to read, there's so much to read that's better, more interesting, more exciting, I keep reading that. I have to force myself to read these books. Whenever we're supposed to read Romeo and Juliet that's when I want to read Jane Austen. When we're supposed to read Andrew Marvell I want to read Isaac Asimov. Have you read Foundation and Empire? It's great. I love reading but I hate school. It's torture. But I have to do it. If only I was free to just read whatever I wanted, just get lost in books and writers and ideas. But you have to come back to the themes of Romeo and Juliet and character in the modern novel and compare and contrast Andrew Marvell and … and a two-headed cow. I'm no good helping you. I'm a fraud Danny. I don't even want to do Law. God, what am I saying? I'm doing it for my mother.

On Your Feet (continued)

Everytime she looks in on me with my desk lamp on and all the books stacked around the desk, I can feel her wanting me to be a genius, to get 501 out of 500 and become the world's greatest lawyer. All I want to do is read a book about something that's not on the course. I'm a fraud. What would be really great would be if they just said read fifty books and see fifty films and go to ten foreign countries and learn ten poems and join a rock group and come back in two years and we'll give you the Higher School Certificate. But we're stuck with this stuff. Cram it in and forget it two days after the exam. Oh let me out of here. I need some air. Hence, knave, avaunt thee outside to thy bike.

(from *All Stops Out*, by Michael Gow)

Props and stage business

A well-chosen prop or a piece of stage business can help in developing your character, and provide options for blocking.

Props can be a great help to the performer. In a monologue, a prop can be utilised to add to the physicality, reveal character and add variety to your performance. Having something specific to do can also minimise the problem of self-consciousness. Similarly, stage business can serve the same purpose. The next improvisation exercise asks you to incorporate an arbitrary prop and a specific piece of 'business'.

Work in small groups of three to four students. Each group is given at random, one scene-starter, one prop (which may be mimed), and a piece of business from the lists below. Allow sufficient time to develop and drill before presentation.

Each group then presents their improvisation. Although the results will be comic, discuss the potential of using props and business as part of your monologue.

Scene starter	Prop	Business
What went wrong at the wedding ceremony	A mobile phone	A Mexican wave
The reading of the will	A Chuppa Chup	A tap dance
Trapped in the lift	A pet rock	Trying to get rid of chewing gum stuck on a finger
The cooking program	An electronic organiser	A persistent mosquito
The queue at the autobank	A walkman	Obsessive knitting

Navigating Drama

Stagecraft

Appreciating drama: Workshop summary

Here is a summary of what was learned in the workshop.
Make a record in your logbook.
- Vocal and physical warm-up exercises can have a beneficial effect on developing your monologue. Warming up your mind is equally important.
- Using references is a technique to help you mean what you say on stage.
- A well-chosen prop or a piece of stage business can help in developing your character and providing options for movement on stage.

Now describe the workshop from your point of view.
- Why do you think these particular warm-up exercises were chosen for this workshop?
- What are the advantages for an actor of 'using references'?
- Which prop and stage business was your group assigned? Describe how you developed the impro. Did the performance go as expected?

The performance

When performing a monologue, you will be alone on the stage.

The time you spend in front of an audience is when you will do most of your learning about the art of acting. No amount of intellectualising and guess-work can substitute for the practical experience of performing.

Hard Times,
Ensemble Theatre.

Stagecraft

Performing drama: Coping with nerves

Read through and make your own notes in your logbook about what to do about nerves.

Nerves are part of performance.

In spite of what you may hear people say, everyone experiences some form of nervousness when performing in public. What is important is how you deal with it.

Everyone is different. Some actors will combat performance nerves by doing rigorous warm-up exercises to focus their concentration. Others will do breathing and relaxation exercises. Some will divert themselves by talking to anyone about anything. Experiment with what works for you.

Don't discuss with your fellow actors (assuming that your monologue is part of a larger evening's entertainment) about how nervous you are or aren't feeling. They may have been coping quite well with their own nerves until you reminded them.

If, in spite of everything, you find yourself swamped by nerves as you are about to go on, there is one vital thing to remember: Don't panic.
Try one or more of the following measures:
- Use your acting skills to turn your fears into positive, non-threatening thoughts.
- Think of the audience as a group of supporters rather than judgmental critics.
- Focus your thoughts on the character you are going to introduce to the audience.
- Remind yourself of all the preparation you have done, and you will realise that no matter what may go wrong, you will cope. You will fall back on the techniques you have learned during rehearsal, and you will come up with the goods.
- Dedicate your performance to someone who is important to you. Do it for them, not yourself.

It is quite common to experience dreams about the performance near the end of rehearsals. Common dreams centre on being on stage in the wrong costume or in the wrong play, not knowing the dialogue, not recognising the other characters on stage, speaking a different language to the other actors, and so on. Don't be disturbed by these dreams; they are an absolutely normal and healthy occurrence.

Stagecraft

Performing drama: Coping with audience reaction

Read through and make your own notes in your logbook about what to do about audience reaction.

Hopefully you will be able to practise your monologue as often as possible in front of friends, teachers and members of the public. This is the best way of testing and refining your work.

Although it is true that your focus in performance should be on what you are doing on stage, a small part of your concentration should be on what is happening around you. If your powers of concentration are so intense that you do not hear the audience laugh, and you continue talking; or you do not hear someone shout 'Fire!' and carry on with great authority as the building blazes around you, you have a problem!

As much as we might desire it to be otherwise, a small part of your focus as an actor in performance must include an awareness of the audience.

Audiences can be contrary beasts. Audience members will cough, laugh, arrive late, leave, talk, fidget and generally seem as if they are trying their utmost to disturb your concentration and upset your timing and phrasing. But this is the reality of live performance; the audience is the other essential side of the performance equation.

However, there are tricks and techniques you can use to assist you in the battle with this friendly giant.

- Commonsense is the primary requirement. If you become aware of a problem – adjust. If a torrential downpour occurs – speak up until it subsides. If you hear whisperings from the audience of 'What was that?', the odds are your volume is not loud enough.
- If you drop something – pick it up.
- If you trip on a rug – stop, look at the rug, straighten it. Provided you remain in character, you can cope with any mishaps that occur, and make them part of the action.
- Don't continue to speak when laughter occurs. If you do, the dialogue will not be heard. The audience may become confused. In addition, if the audience senses that it is not being given time to react, it will not react at all, which is a definite problem if you are involved in a comedy.
- If the audience laughs, continue to play the previous action until you sense the laugh receding. You can also signal that you are about to go on with a slight physical movement before beginning to speak. If you observe stand-up comics delivering a routine, you will see how they use these techniques to control laughter and manipulate it to their advantage.
- If you do not get a laugh when you expect one, do not worry. No line is intrinsically funny in itself. Stay in character and get on with the scene.
- Avoid the temptation to play solely for laughs; you run the risk of sacrificing the content and characterisation, and spoiling the monologue.
- Don't expect that your performance will produce the same reactions in different audiences. Every audience is unique and will react to different things. Some audiences will enjoy a comic monologue immensely, but not express their enjoyment overtly. They may be smiling loudly.
- Learn to cherish and savour the differences between audiences, and the fact that every performance will be different.

Notes

Scripts suitable for monologues (page 141)

The lines spoken by Vickie in the first passage would probably not make a successful monologue. Her speech is merely the retelling of a story, and this is not enough for an effective piece of theatre. We are not given any real clues about Vickie's character in these lines, nor do we know her relationship with either David or Tom.

Without knowing anything about the play from which it is taken, both performer and audience will find the second passage more accessible. Colin Brunner's objective is clear – to dress down the members of his team. The audience is addressed directly; the tone is confronting, suggesting a high energy level, and the character is strongly drawn.

Which piece would make the most effective monologue? Passage two. It speaks directly to the audience. A performer should also aim to include some light and shade within the passage, to prevent it from becoming a harangue.

Identifying conflict (page 143)

The first passage deals with a straightforward form of conflict. Here, an Aboriginal boy challenges his white friends with some information that has come into his hands about a historical incident in which some Aboriginal people were poisoned. He is outraged, and cries out in anger.

In Passage two, Sloane lightheartedly reveals the details of a murder he has committed. What do you think the writer intended his audience to feel about this character? Should they understand his violent behaviour? Should they be horrified by it? Here the conflict lies between the character's tone, which is created by Sloane's attitude towards what he is saying, and the way the audience feels about what he is telling them. The gentler and more offhand Sloane's tone is, the more horrifying the effect on the audience.

Clearly drawn characters (page 145)

The first passage gives a vivid picture of Dave's father, but contains few clues about the character of Dave himself. You would need to study the play to find more information about him, so it would be difficult to play this character convincingly from just this excerpt.

In the second passage, Aggie is written as a three dimensional character. As she recounts a simple episode of being lost in Sydney, we have a clear picture of her family, her situation, her relationship with her husband, her view of the world, and her emotional state.

Unit assessment

Performing drama: Developing and performing a monologue

(Four to six lessons' preparation.)

- Choose a suitable monologue.
- Research and interpret your character.
- Choreograph your blocking.
- Learn the dialogue.
- Duration three to five minutes.

In your logbook

- Keep a lesson-by-lesson account of your process.
- Include a character profile and character history.
- Do the appropriate research.
- Include an annotated script containing blocking and any other relevant information.
- Complete a post-performance self-evaluation discussing the strengths of the project from your point of view.

Assessment criteria

- Can understand and manipulate the elements of drama
- Use of voice and physicality in presentation of character
- Ability to engage with an audience in a way that is appropriate to the style
- Ability to record the process of rehearsal and performance
- Analysis of the process, and self-evaluation

Assessment feedback sheet

Developing and performing a monologue

	Level of Achievement				
	Developing		Substantial		Excellent

Performance

Use of voice and physicality in creating a character	1	2	3	4	5
Appropriate and effective staging	1	2	3	4	5
Audience engagement	1	2	3	4	5

Logbook

Completes entries for each session	1	2	3	4	5
Analysis and reflection about your work	1	2	3	4	5
Post-performance self-evaluation	1	2	3	4	5

Teacher's comments

_____
_____
_____
_____
_____
_____
_____

Student's comments on their strengths, as well as areas that need more work, thought and attention

_____
_____
_____
_____
_____
_____
_____

Chapter 7

Scriptwriting

Outcomes

In this topic you will:

- recognise and manipulate the elements of scriptwriting
- give shape to a dramatic scene
- explore character and relationships through written dialogue
- develop linear scene and plot structures and incorporate them into a script.

What is a script?

A drama script consists of people talking.

But what sort of talking?

If you were to listen to two people chatting on a train after work one evening you might overhear something like this:

Joe: G'day, Frank.
Frank: Hi, Joe.
Joe: How ya goin'?
Frank: Oh, you know.
Joe: Yeah.
Frank: Can't complain.
Joe: 'Nother day another dollar!
Frank: Ha, ha.

This sort of conversation takes place everywhere, but it does not make interesting stage dialogue. It is dull and full of cliches. We do not want to sit and listen to this kind of thing in the theatre. Dramatic dialogue must be entertaining and interesting.

Joe: How's things, Frank?
Frank: Joe. Come here. Remember what I told you yesterday?
Joe: About your naturopath?
Frank: It's true.
Joe: No!
Frank: Would I lie to you?
Joe: That's terrible, Frank!
Frank: So I ...
Joe: You didn't, did you?
Frank: I certainly did!

This conversation is more interesting. These two men know what they are talking about, but we do not. The trouble with this as stage dialogue is that it does not give us enough information. Stage dialogue is not the same thing as realistic conversation. Stage dialogue needs to be clear.

Joe: How ya goin', Frank?
Frank: Hell, Joe, I've been having these pains in my stomach again which were playing up last summer. Went to a naturopath this time and he put me on this stuff, what's it called? Oh, you know, begins with M. Minki something. Moley ... Got a picture of flowers on the front. Never mind, doesn't matter, but I tried it only last week and it was a – Molkosan! That's it. I've been having trouble remembering things, names of things, you know, just lately, never happened before. Mind like a steel clamp, George used to say, 'Frank's got a mind like a steel clamp'. Anyway, Maud's convinced it's old age, but I keep tellin' her she's three days older than me! When I first met her I told my father I was marrying an older woman ... Dad nearly had a fit! Ha, ha. Eh?
Joe: That reminds me, Frank ...

It is clear what these two people are talking about, but their conversation does not make effective stage dialogue. It is too full of irrelevant information and it jumps about all over the place.

Stage dialogue must necessarily be concentrated.

This dialogue does not do any of the three things that stage dialogue must do. Stage dialogue must have a purpose, and that means that it must either:
- create atmosphere
- reveal character or
- advance the plot.

Joe: Frank, you look terrible!
Frank: She's trying to kill me, Joe.
Joe: Who? Maud?
Frank: I've got proof.
Joe: Don't be silly, Frank.
Frank: She and that naturopath. They're poisoning me.
Joe: They're helping you, Frank. Those medicines may not taste nice but they do you good.
Frank: I pour it down the sink, you know. I'm too clever for them.

This dialogue works. It is interesting and clear. It is economic, saying more in eight lines than two people might normally say in as much natural conversation. (Stage characters are more articulate and exaggerated than real-life people.) These men are *communicating*.

Characters must do more than talk, they must engage with each other.

Finally, this dialogue has purpose: it gives us an insight into the characters of the two men, and it advances the plot.

Stagecraft

Appreciating drama: Evaluating dialogue

Examine these three pieces of stage dialogue. Which one is the best? Give detailed reasons for your choice. Write notes in your logbook discussing all three excerpts, showing clearly the limitations of those pieces you do not consider to be so successful.

1   A: You're frightened, aren't you?
    B: Am I?
    A: You find me attractive?
    B: I'm old enough to be your father.
    A: That's not what I asked.
    B: I've a daughter your age.
    A: You're married. I thought so. I can tell the type.
    B: Can you?
    A: Yes. Tired. Unadventurous. You're in a rut. I suppose you've done the same job all your life.
    B: As a matter of fact, I have.
    A: There you are. People like you don't know what life's all about. You're dead before you begin. That's not the sort of life for me. I want to be free. You wouldn't know the meaning of the word. I want to travel and feel the wind in my hair. I don't want to end up like you.

Navigating Drama

2   A: You knew they wouldn't hold up in the air.
    B: I didn't say that.
    A: But you were going to warn them not to use them –
    B: But that don't mean –
    A: It means you knew they'd crash.
    B: It don't mean that.
    A: Then you thought they'd crash.
    B: I was afraid maybe –
    A: You were afraid maybe! God in heaven, what kind of a man are you? Kids were hanging in the air by those heads. You knew that!
    B: For you, a business for you.
    A: For me! Where do you live, where have you come from? For me! I was dying every day and you were killing my boys and you did it for me? What the hell do you think I was thinking of, the goddam business? Is that as far as your mind can see, the business? What is that, the world – the business? What the hell do you mean, you did it for me? Don't you have a country? Don't you live in the world?

3   A: Where do you think you're going?
    B: Out.
    A: Oh no you don't.
    B: Are you going to stop me?
    A: I'm going to stand by this door until you sit down and take off your coat.
    B: It stays on, Ethel.
    A: I mean it. I'm not moving.
    B: Get out of my way. I'm warning you. I've got a bottle in my hand.
    A: I'm staying put.
    B: I'm coming over. Don't say I didn't warn you.

When you have completed this activity, turn to the *Notes* on page 182.

Deeds,
Ensemble Theatre.

The indirect approach

Because characters can be seen on the stage, they do not have to tell the audience what they are doing.

In the same way they do not have to tell the audience what they are talking about, they just talk. One of the tricks of writing dialogue is to reveal the characters, their motives, and the mood and plot of the play, while the characters are *actually talking about something else.*

Never let characters ask questions to get information; all information should be revealed naturally during the course of the conversation.

Look at the first lines of *A Doctor in Spite of Himself* by Molière:

Sganarelle: No, I tell you I'll have nothing to do with it and it's for me to say. I'm the master.
Martine: And I'm telling you that I'll have you do as I want. I didn't marry you to put up with your nonsensical goings on.

Sganarelle: Oh! The misery of married life! How right Aristotle was when he said wives were the very devil!

Martine: Just listen to the clever fellow – him and his blockhead of an Aristotle!

Sganarelle: Yes, I'm a clever fellow all right! Show me a woodcutter who can argue and hold forth like me, a man who has served six years with a famous physician and had his Latin grammar off by heart from infancy!

Martine: A plague on the idiot!

Sganarelle: A plague on you, you worthless hussy!

Martine: A curse on the day and hour when I took it into my head to go and say 'I will'!

Sganarelle: And a curse on the cuckold of a priest who made me sign my name to my own ruin.

Martine: A lot of reason you have to complain, I must say! You ought to thank Heaven every minute of your life that you have me for a wife. Do you think you deserved to marry a woman like me?

Sganarelle: It's true you did me a great honour and I had good cause to be satisfied with my wedding night, but confound it! Don't set me talking about that – I might say things …

From these lines we learn that Sganarelle is a woodcutter and Martine is his wife. Their relationship is full of bombast, argument and rivalry, but one senses from Sganarelle's vulgar remarks that there is an understanding between them.

Remember: *Characters do not always say what they think.*

Sganarelle and Martine are partners. Sganarelle is vain and proud of his limited education; Martine is not the slightest bit impressed. Sganarelle is a bully; Martine is his equal. Sganarelle is rude, self-indulgent and loquacious; Martine has a sharp tongue in her head, and a brain as well.

The mood of the play is energetic, and we can see from the first line that it is a comedy. Molière is concentrating on making the conflict amusing, but he reveals his information indirectly to the audience as he does so.

Stagecraft

Making drama: Short dialogue exercises

For each of these exercises write a short section of stage dialogue for two people. The characters speak in turns. Write twelve lines, each character speaking six. Work in your logbook.

1. The characters must talk about travel. In the course of the dialogue they must reveal who they are and what their relationship is.
2. The characters must talk about music. In the course of the dialogue they must each reveal five things about themselves.
3. The characters must talk about money. In the course of the dialogue they must reveal who they are, where they are, what their relationship is and create a definite mood.
4. The characters must talk about the weather. In the course of the dialogue they must reveal who they are, where they are and that they have only just met. They must also introduce a plot.

5   The characters must talk about food. In the course of the dialogue they must reveal that it's winter in Sydney, Australia and the date is 1798. One character is frightened, and the other does not sense this.
6   The characters must talk about Shakespeare. One of the characters is a policeman who has just lost a brother in the war. The other character is a burglar who keeps looking for an opportunity to make a hasty exit. It must be amusing.

The Lieutenant of Inishmore, Belvoir St Theatre, Company B.

Cliched dialogue

Avoid cliches in your stage dialogue.

If characters speak in cliches then they become caricatures. These people are easily recognised; for example:
- The teenager who becomes angry at the slightest provocation and storms out of the room slamming the door.
- The overly-concerned mother who dabs her eyes in the kitchen, wondering where she went wrong.
- The drunk in the park, wearing a raincoat and carrying a bottle of port concealed in a brown paper bag.

Cliched dialogue turns people into cardboard cut-outs.

Actors do not enjoy playing cliched roles; it is hard to give a character any depth if the dialogue is superficial. Actors enjoy playing complex characters, changeable characters, people you can believe in.

Believable characters speak with their own voice. Their registers and rhythms are distinctive. No two people will use language in exactly the same way.

A good test is to read a line from your script and ask yourself, 'Could anyone have spoken this line?'. If the answer is 'Yes', then you may have to think about rewriting it.

Female writers (particularly) should avoid this kind of thing:
- *Thanks for always being there, Sal. You're a beautiful person.*
- *Mum hardly even knows I exist.*
- *If you've got it, flaunt it!*
- *Why our baby? Why our little Mia? Why, God, oh why?*
- *It's in the past and I've put it behind me.*
- *I was like Wow!*

Male writers (particularly) should beware of this sort of thing:
- *I don't need this!*
- *Dad hardly even knows I exist!*
- *Either you got it or you don't!*
- *You give me the shits!*
- *It's something I have to do ...*
- *She was like Wow!*

Stagecraft

Appreciating, making and performing drama:
Scene of cliched dialogue

Make your own list of cliches.

Collect them from school, home, TV soaps, the radio, magazines and newspapers. When you have collected several hundred of them, write a short scene in your logbook for two or three characters using only lines from your list.

Perform the scene.

Tricks of the trade

Dramatic action

Dramatic action is the activity that sustains a play. Dramatic action is anything that happens on-stage, that reveals character, builds the mood, or advances the plot. Dramatic action can happen during a shouting match, or it can happen in silence. When writing a script, the playwright must always envisage the dramatic action that accompanies the dialogue. People laugh, fall in love, go to work, argue, tell lies, betray each other, and refuse to face up to reality. They slam doors, climb balconies, dress up in other people's clothing, eat cucumber sandwiches, and throw things at each other. They even, at times, kill each other.

You should think carefully before including a death in your play. If you decide that a death is necessary, then lead up to it skilfully. A sudden death can be amusing rather than tragic if not handled properly. Sometimes a sad and lonely character, left alive and suffering, can be more tragic than a dead one. An audience might identify with such a person.

Sensational material should be handled with care. These subjects include AIDS, schizophrenia, homosexuality, anorexia, incest, rape, drug overdose, teenage suicide, horrible parents, car accidents, senile dementia and madness. The temptation is to be melodramatic. To tackle these subjects head-on can often result in clumsy and embarrassing scripting.

Good scripts are often about characters responding to things that have happened, rather than about characters making things happen. Thus it is probably a better idea to explore the effects of a drug overdose on close friends of the victim rather than trying to portray the party scene where the overdose actually took place. It is more effective to show a group of students reacting to a friend's suicide than trying to portray the messy event itself.

In theatre, a dramatic moment is often:
- an unexpected revelation (as when, for example, one character is revealed as being someone else)
- a sudden insight (as when we abruptly realise how desperate a character really is) or
- an unexpected twist of plot (as when we suddenly understand that a basic situation is not what we had believed it to be).

It does not need to be a gruesome rape or a horrible and violent death.

Theatre and film

Most people watch a lot of film and television, but do not go to the theatre very often. Because film and theatre both deal with dramatic events, it is easy to assume that they are pretty much the same thing. This is not true.

The basic unit of a play is the scene, which usually has a dramatic structure of its own. The basic unit of a film is the shot, which does not. In film the dramatic effect is achieved by the cutting together of shots.

A scene is generally a more sustained piece of work than a shot. When creating a realistic dramatic scene you need to develop a situation slowly and carefully. A scene often requires more dialogue than first envisaged. A theatre audience will get irritated if there are many short, superficial scenes with lots of scene changes; they will lose concentration and interest.

Theatre is more static than film. Whereas a film can transport you from a tropical island in the Pacific to a Melbourne backstreet in seconds, a realistic play can not. A whole scene, sometimes even a whole play, may be set in the one place.

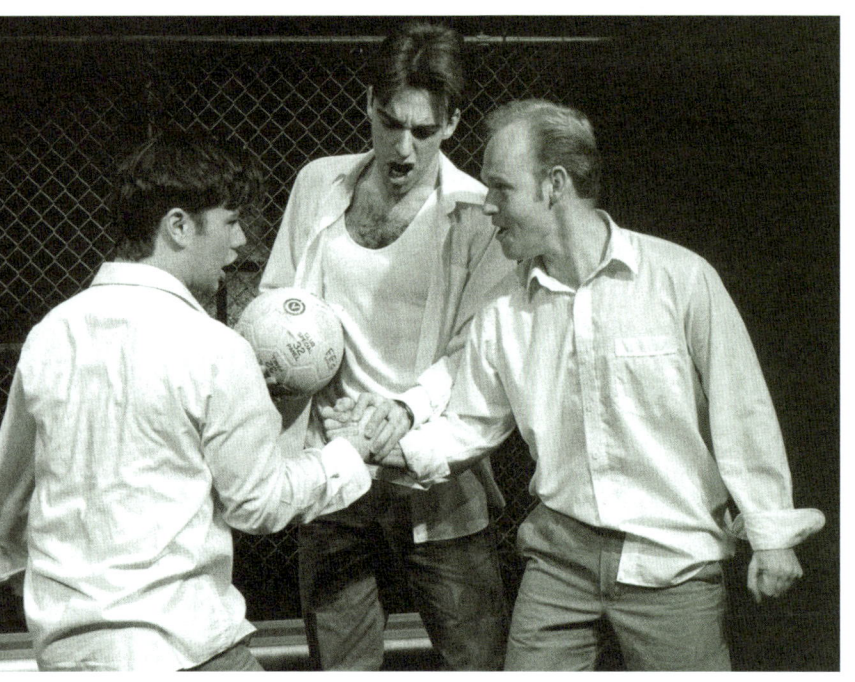

The Heartbreak Kid, Ensemble Theatre.

Stagecraft

Appreciating drama: Stage limitations

Which of these scenes do you think could be satisfactorily presented on a stage, and which could not? In your logbook, discuss the reasons for your conclusions.
- A car chase
- A tea party
- A scene where a man gets eaten by a shark
- A bar room scene

- A bar room fight scene
- A bushfire scene
- A childbirth scene in a hospital
- A scene set inside a lift
- A scene set on the moon

If you are putting together a realistic piece of theatre on war, it is better to set your scene in a dugout, where people can talk, rather than recreating World War Two on the stage, where it will not fit.

It is important to realise that 'dramatic action' does not necessarily mean physical action. A scene full of violence, swearing, chases, punch-ups and people falling off the stage does not make good theatre. As a general rule, it is a good idea to use violent physical action sparingly on stage. When you do use it, choreograph it well. Big-budget physical action is the stuff of film and television.

When working on a script, 'think theatre' and go and see plays. Cut down on watching film and television.

Inspiration

Personal experience is a good source of ideas. Anything can be transformed into a play, and incidents from your own life (or from the lives of people you know) can form the basis of a successful script. It is a good idea, however, to distance yourself from your experiences as you write, to get some objectivity into your work. Without this, the dangers are that such a script might rely on emotion rather than plot, and the conflict could be clumsy or unbalanced.

Do not use your script as an excuse to preach, or as a source of revenge.

Stagecraft
Making drama: Finding a plot

The best sources of ideas for plays are newspapers, magazines and photographs (far better than television). Read them, looking for stories or plots that capture your interest. Don't just look at the sensational stories, but search out the human-interest pieces.

Over the period of a week, make a collection of photographs and newspaper and magazine cuttings in your logbook.

At the end of the week select one, and give a talk to the rest of the group, explaining how you might use it in a script. Explain how you could transform the story into a shape of your own by changing the names, altering the angle of the circumstances or playing with the central idea of the piece.

Follow-up discussions are usually revealing and rewarding.

Navigating Drama

Stagecraft

Making drama: Finding characters

In the same way you can collect plots, you can also collect characters. The people in your play might be based on your friends (careful here!), relations (even more careful!), people you have seen on television, people observed in the street, or people taken from newspaper stories. Sometimes you can mix personal qualities from two or more characters to create a character of your own. Remember to write interesting characters into your play, characters you would like to act yourself.

Collect six character studies in your logbook, three men and three women, one to a page. In creating your characters you may use any of the suggestions above. Each character page must contain:
- a photo or drawing of the character
- a full, clear character study
- an explanation of how you 'created' your character.

Start of the play: exposition

Exposition is the art of giving the audience the basic necessary information at the start of the play. They must know:
- when and where the play is set
- who the on-stage characters are
- what their relationships are
- the nature of the main conflict.

All these facts must be given in an interesting fashion.

Sets and costumes will help, but the main way of imparting this information is through dialogue. One approach is to use a chorus. The chorus simply stands centre stage and tells the audience everything they need to know – as if talking to a friend. The Greeks used this direct method of introduction and so, at times, did Shakespeare. Today we associate this practice with the playwright Bertolt Brecht.

The problem of course, in a naturalistic play, is for the exposition to appear realistic. People don't go around spouting facts about themselves and their surroundings in the normal course of events. They talk about other things.

Simpson, J. 202, Ensemble Theatre.

Stagecraft

Making drama: Experiments in exposition

A good idea is to start your play with something that is not within the normal course of events. Try scripting one of the following in your logbook.

- **A brief scene where a character is introducing a stranger to a friend or relative**
  These introductions will seem natural, and the audience will pick up the facts quickly.
- **A brief scene which takes place during a special occasion**
  This gives the on-stage characters something special to talk about because it is new and exciting to them. In speaking about this event they can reveal facts about themselves.
- **A brief scene involving a blazing row**
  This enables characters to say a number of things about themselves and each other that they would otherwise not mention.

Entrances and exits

Entrances and exits are important. When a character walks onto the stage the audience must believe that they have come from somewhere, and are on the stage for some definite purpose. Similarly, when an actor leaves the stage the audience must believe that they have somewhere definite to go to, and a strong reason for doing so. When a character walks onto the stage the audience needs to know who they are. There are two approaches you can take here.

In the direct approach, a character walks onto the stage, addresses the audience and introduces themselves. This is the Brechtian approach. It solves a lot of problems and can be entertaining but it is out of place in a realistic play.

In the indirect approach, the audience is prepared for a character's entrance by an on-stage character. Rather than have someone say, 'My cruel, domineering father should be getting home from his office in the city any moment now' *(enter Dad)*, it is preferable to include something like this:

Mother: Have you finished cleaning the garage, Tom?
Tom: No.
Mother: You'd better have it done before your father gets back!

That is enough. The audience is alerted to the boy's father and will recognise him when he appears.

As a general rule, characters should not stand about too long on the stage without speaking. If they have no business on stage, get them off.

Exit lines, like entrance lines, are important. Exit lines should be strong. Shakespeare used rhyming couplets to give a dramatic flourish to an exit:

> *Hear it not, Duncan; for it is a knell*
> *That summons thee to Heaven or to Hell.*

(Macbeth)

In *The Club* by David Williamson, Danny leaves the stage with a threat:

> *You watch the way you talk to me in future, Parker, or you'll end up getting flattened!*

Shouts, screams or roars of laughter can create effective exits.

Exit lines can be strong without being loud or violent. Look at Nora's exit at the end of *A Doll's House* by Henrik Ibsen.

A Doll's House rehearsal, Sydney Theatre Company.

End of the play: Conclusion

Endings are important. When members of the audience leave the theatre, it is the final scene of the play that will remain in their minds. This scene might be tragic, thought provoking or amusing, but it is always important.

Experience will help you understand what makes a good ending. But a play must have a plot, and its main conflict should be resolved in the final scene. A play should come to a strong ending rather than a sudden stop.

Endings must be believable.

One sort of ending that does not work is that based on coincidence or luck; one in which the solution to the problems in the play is provided by forces outside the drama. The Greeks called this *deus ex machina*, a technique by which a god descended on a crane from above to sort out the complications of the play. An example of this might be a situation in which a middle-aged man is struggling to provide for his family. He has a mortgage, his wife is sick, and it looks as though he is going to lose his job. For the entire play we witness him wrestling with these problems, until, in the final act he wins Tatts Lotto and all is rosy. Although this is perfectly possible (someone must win Tatts Lotto!) an audience does not find it satisfying.

In the same way, it is not a good idea to introduce a new character, in the dying moments of a play, with important information that solves a mystery or gets the hero out of jail. The solutions to a play's complications must come from *within* the drama.

A good ending to a play is often surprising yet inevitable; a seeming paradox.

On Your Feet

Scriptwriting: Workshop

Relaxation

Relaxation is one of the keys to effective work in drama.

- Lie on the floor of a darkened room or with your eyes closed. Become aware of the places where your body touches the ground. Breathe deeply, in through your nose, out through your mouth.
- Become aware of the tension in your body. Stretch, then relax, each part of your body isolating them in turn: toes, ankles, legs, fingers, wrists and arms, lifting them off the floor as you do so. Sit up. Roll your shoulders backwards, forwards, then roll both shoulders together in opposite directions. Let your head drop onto your chest. Roll it slowly (and carefully) around your shoulders.
- Lie down again. Eyes closed. Let the day's tensions seep away. Breathe the positive in and the negative out. You are recreating yourself as a blank page.

On Your Feet (continued)

Games for developing dialogue
These games demonstrate various ways that dialogue can be developed. Scriptwriters: take note!

Wrong number
In this exercise the performers are not able to see who they are talking to. This focuses attention on to the dialogue.
- Still lying on the floor of a darkened room or with eyes closed. Create a character in your head: decide on the age, sex, nationality, accent, religion, married status, work, hobbies, political attitudes, of your character. Finally, decide on a reason for making a telephone call.
- Two student names are called out. The first rings the second. No action takes place. Everyone listens to the phone conversation. Of course it will be a wrong number. Don't hang up. Find a way of developing a conversation with someone you have never met and cannot see. Finally, ring off. Repeat with two other performers.
- Afterwards, sit up and discuss your findings.

Bus stop
This game helps actors with their entrance and exit lines.
- Two characters, A and B, are standing at a bus stop. They talk. They are then joined by C. C must find a realistic first line. The three talk, until A, tired of waiting, leaves. A must find a realistic exit line. Soon B and C are joined by D. D must find a realistic first line. After a while B leaves. B must find a realistic exit line. This continues until everyone has had a turn.
- Keep the conversation flowing, interesting and varied. Afterwards, discuss what works and what doesn't. If you are a keen playwright, take notes.
- The bus never comes.

Hiding the lines
This game forces performers to make the unexpected believable, and to search for dialogue outside their comfort zone.
- Each student is privately given one outlandish sentence. Two performers are then called out to enact a conversation (interviews work well here) in front of the rest of the group. The task is for each of them to include their own given sentence into the conversation without it seeming to be out of place, and without it being spotted by the audience.
- Sentences could include such things as:
  - 'I have a pet rattlesnake'
  - 'They fell for each other on the leaning tower of Pisa'
  - 'I gather you're a sex symbol, Reg'
  - 'He was mugged in Perth, obviously'
  - 'She is an out-of-work balloon sculptress'
  - 'I'm trying to learn Italian, not run a branch-line railway service'.

Power-play improvisations
This exercise forces players to find the words and methods with which to pursue their separate objectives.
- Two actors take the stage. They are each privately handed a piece of paper. On each is written an objective. Neither sees the other's objective. Without any preparation they must improvise a scene, each trying to fulfil their own objective. Set a time limit of five minutes. There will be a winner and a loser. Here are some suggestions.
- It is their wedding anniversary.
  - SHE is upset because her husband has forgotten about it, and is *determined* to make him take her out to dinner.
  - HE had planned a night out with the boys and is *determined* not to miss it.
- A young man is applying for a teacher's job.
  - The YOUNG MAN has excellent qualifications and is *determined* to get the job.
  - The HEADMISTRESS does not like men very much and is *determined* not to employ one.
- A young wife has arranged for her lover, the local butcher, to come over while her husband is at evening classes.
  - The HUSBAND returns early, classes cancelled, *determined* to spend a relaxing evening with his wife.
  - SHE is *determined* to get rid of him before the butcher arrives. She has five minutes.

Navigating Drama

Stagecraft

Appreciating drama: Some questions

Here are a dozen don'ts. Why do you think scriptwriters are advised to observe these rules? Write your answers in your logbook.

1. Don't write scripts with excessively large casts.
2. Don't write scripts with animals in them.
3. Don't write plays with too many telephone conversations in them.
4. Don't write scripts which ask the actors to make up some of their own lines.
5. Don't write complicated speeches for actors to speak from off-stage.
6. Don't write overly long sentences.
7. Don't write tongue-twisters.
8. Don't write two lines exactly the same.
9. Don't write scripts where characters have similar sounding names, or where all their names start with the same letter.
10. Don't write plays full of topical allusions, local references, foreign accents or slang expressions.
11. Don't explain the plot in the program.
12. Don't take any of these don'ts as gospel truth.

Making the lines work

A playwright must develop an instinct for the structure of dialogue. It is not enough to write down lines and assume that they are working. *There is a direct connection between the subject matter of a scene and the length of script needed to carry that subject matter.* Generally speaking, an effective script feeds lines to an audience in a way that makes the message clear. Stage dialogue is like a river; it must flow evenly. If there is a torrent then the audience will be confused; if the stream becomes a trickle then the audience will get bored. The flow of dialogue must be carefully controlled.

The Hanging Man rehearsal, Sydney Theatre Company.

Stagecraft

Appreciating and making drama: Dialogue flow

Examine this piece of dialogue.

Claudia: I'm sorry, Margot, but I'm going to have to let you go.

Margot: You're firing me, Claudia?

Claudia: That's right, Margot. The market is in a bad state at present. When I employed you things were different. I only took you on because you are my brother's wife. Martin made me do it. The truth is, you've never fitted in with the rest of the girls. You keep yourself to yourself. I have to say, I won't miss you.

Claudia's second speech would confuse an audience because there are seven different ideas in it. A general rule to observe is to include only one idea per speech. Audiences digest material slowly. With scripted dialogue you cannot flick back, as you can with a novel, to catch up on something you have missed.

Rewrite this scene in your logbook, controlling the dialogue flow.

Stage setting

The stage setting should also be clearly described at the start of the play. The important thing about a set is that it must work. Plays take place somewhere, and it is a good idea to build a model of your set, and move figures around on it beforehand to determine the spaces, the sightlines and so on. It should be possible to sketch a set from the description of the stage setting.

Set design by Derrick Cox for *One for the Road*, Ensemble Theatre.

Navigating Drama

Stagecraft

Appreciating drama: Stage settings

Draw the following stage settings in your logbook. What are your conclusions? What is practical, and what is not? Give detailed reasons for your views.

1. The stage is divided between the Bradshaw's living room and Roger's bedroom. The bedroom is stage-right, the living room stage-left. The bedroom is empty except for Roger's bed, which stands downstage. The back wall of this half of the stage is painted white, and at various times during the play Roger's nightmares will be projected onto this backdrop. The living room contains a sofa in the centre of the room, with two large comfortable chairs at either side of it. There is a coffee table downstage centre, and a large bookshelf upstage. A lamp stands stage-left of the sofa. There is no wall between the two rooms, but a suspended doorframe upstage is used for characters to pass from one room to the next.

2. The stage is roughly square; one of the corners of the square juts out into the audience as an apron stage. The audience sits along the two sides of this square. The other corner of the square lies upstage, the two on-stage sides being a solid construction representing castellated towers, city walls and so on. It is possible to walk along the tops of these 'walls', which form a continual upper acting area. A broad set of steps, circular at the foot, and filling in the whole ninety degrees, leads up from the stage to the upstage juncture of the walls. These steps are broad, and can be used as acting areas. There are two large wooden doors, one set in each wall. Downstage centre stands an imposing throne. It never moves, and is the only bit of furniture on the stage.

Stage directions

Insertions, comments and clarifications made by the playwright during the course of the action are called stage directions. These are usually written in italics and placed in brackets.

Stage directions should be clear, helpful, and brief. They should **not** be vague or ambiguous. Some examples of stage directions that are **not** helpful:

- *John gives Annabel a look that says more than a thousand words.*
- *Mary walks towards Pearl, and both women share the joy of their children.*
- *Jeff moves into a separate reality.*
- *As Julian dies, all the birds stop singing.*
- *The men discuss cars for the next twenty minutes.*
- *Captain Bligh loses consciousness as his rowing boat is tossed about in the Indian Ocean.*
- *The curtain opens to reveal a dark stage.*
- *Eric has a flashback.*
- *Scene 1: Diana is born.*
  Scene 2: A couple of years later. Diana is now five years old.

Use stage directions sparingly. Do not interrupt the play unless it is really necessary. Most directors will probably ignore the directions anyway. They are not law, they are just clarifications and suggestions.

Structuring the scene

Theatre is not storytelling.

A play is not a novel with the narrative sections taken out. An audience will not sit still on uncomfortable seats for two hours if all that is being offered is a story. They can go and read stories for themselves in their own time.

When a public speaker says: 'I am now going to make six important points about this topic', or 'I'll have more to say about that later on', there is an audible groan from the audience. The speaker has made them aware that they are sitting in a hall, and will probably be there for a long while. They feel trapped. A good speaker will weave some sort of magic through the talk, to make the audience forget about time and place. It will then become theatre.

When the cry of 'Fight!' goes up in the schoolyard, everybody runs to see what is happening. That is theatre. A Grand Final is theatre. Bush fires raging through Sydney is theatre. The opening ceremony of the Olympics is theatre. In other words, there is an immediacy about theatre. The audience has to watch. Something is happening now and it cannot be missed.

How does a play script achieve this?

How should a scene be structured?

Look at this scene from *Away* by Michael Gow. It is Christmas morning, and the family of mum (Gwen), dad (Jim) and daughter (Meg) are camping in their caravan by the beach.

Jim: Has anyone seen a little carton?
Gwen: No.
Jim: A cardboard carton about so big.
Gwen: What carton?
Jim: One of those cartons you bring home from the supermarket. I kept it from going out in the garbage.
Gwen: I haven't seen it.
Jim: Not when we unpacked?
Gwen: No.
Jim: It must be somewhere.
Gwen: What do you need a cardboard carton for?
Meg: What was in it?
Jim: Oh ... something.
Gwen: You packed the car.
Jim: I was sure I left it with the cases.
Gwen: Well, I didn't see any cartons, cardboard or otherwise.
Jim: Don't tell me it didn't come with us. It can't have been left behind.
Gwen: Well, what was in it that was so important?
Jim: You sure you haven't seen it?
Gwen: Do you want to search the place?
Jim: It must have come. Oh, no.
Meg: What was in it?
Jim: All my presents for you. I hid them in a little carton and put it with all the other stuff so you wouldn't notice it.

Gwen:	Oh, well, it looks like you hid them a bit too well. That's a shame. Well, we may as well have what's left of Christmas anyway. Margaret, Merry Christmas. These are the books you'll need. This one's underwear. Jim, there are your socks. That's your fishing reel. I hope it's the one you asked for. Merry Christmas.
Jim:	I can't believe it. How did it happen? I'm sorry.
Gwen:	Now don't go throwing the wrapping paper everywhere. I'm not spending the day chasing wrapping paper all over the State. Though it doesn't look like there'll be much this year.
Jim:	I hid them in a cardboard box. I left it with the suitcases so it would just get packed, no questions asked, and you wouldn't suspect and look inside.
Gwen:	That backfired. And we go without Christmas. *(To Meg)* Are you going to hand yours over? Or can I go and start lunch?
Meg:	Here you are. Merry Christmas.
Gwen:	Thanks. Are these the..?
Meg:	Yes, the plastic mugs.
Gwen:	Marvellous. Thank you. I won't unwrap them all here. And what did you get?
Jim:	Just a little cardboard box.
Gwen:	I think your needle's stuck. What have you got?
Meg:	It's that fishing book.
Gwen:	Oh, that's nice.
Jim:	So big it was.
Gwen:	I'm not going to stand here nattering.
Meg:	I saw the carton.
Jim:	Don't worry, it doesn't matter.
Meg:	I saw it in the hall.
Jim:	Drop it sweetheart.
Meg:	I saw it. It was near the telephone table, wasn't it?
Jim:	That's right but it doesn't matter now.
Gwen:	Christmas is only for the young ones, anyway. I don't know why we bother any more.
Jim:	I was just so sure it would get packed.
Gwen:	I can start cutting up the vegies, I suppose.
Meg:	You saw it too, didn't you? You saw the box sitting there.
Gwen:	I did no such thing.
Meg:	You must have. It was sitting next to your vanity case.
Gwen:	I didn't see any cardboard carton.
Meg:	Everything else that was in the hall got packed in the car. You did see it.
Gwen:	Don't argue with me.
Meg:	You were the last one out. You're the one who shuts the door, after you've made sure the stove's off and the fridge has been left open. You saw the carton and you left it there on purpose.
Gwen:	I most certainly did not.
Meg:	You left it behind.
Jim:	I'll make it up. I'll take us all to the pub for lunch.
Gwen:	You won't get me into that stinking pub.
Meg:	And you knew what it was. You knew what was in it and you left it there.

Gwen:	I will not be accused outside my own caravan. On Christmas morning.
Meg:	Why did you do that?
Gwen:	I'm not on trial.
Meg:	Why would you do a thing like that?
Jim:	Well, it's done now. What's done is done.
Meg:	I want to know why you did it.
Gwen:	You watch your tongue, my girl.
Meg:	Tell me why you deliberately left that box behind.
Jim:	Don't speak to your mother like that.
Meg:	We have a game we play every year. We sneak presents home, we hide them, we wrap them up in secret even though we can hear the sticky tape tearing and the paper rustling; we hide them in the stuff we take away, we pretend not to see them until Christmas morning even when we know they're there and we know what's in them because we've already put in our orders so there's no waste or surprise. And Dad always hides his in a pathetic place that's so obvious it's a joke and we all laugh at him behind his back but we play along! You knew what was in that box. You left it behind. I want to know why.
Gwen:	Where have you picked up these ugly manners?
Meg:	What were you trying to do, what did you want to gain?
Jim:	It's only old presents. Slippers and your new bread knife.
Meg:	Did you want to have something we'd all have to be sorry for the whole holiday? There's always something we do wrong that takes you weeks to forgive.
Gwen:	Where did you learn to say all this?
Meg:	You have to tell me.
Gwen:	The things that are taken away on holidays always go in the proper order, so everything will fit. I can't help it if someone decides to be smart and funny and try to hide things in a little cardboard box. I wasn't going to have the whole routine upset, that we've been following all these years and that I thought was giving people a good life, though it seems I'm very wrong, for the sake of someone's joke.
Meg:	But to do it deliberately!
Gwen:	You're developing a nasty streak. A very nasty, cruel streak. You know what you're becoming? Snide. A nasty, snide girl. No one likes a snide girl, always arguing, always throwing a tantrum, getting your own way, answering back, correcting people, criticising, complaining, no one likes that sort of girl. Unless you count your foulmouthed little English chum. You'll make a great pair. Throw your future away. Give it away. Throw what I have done, we have done, in our faces.
Meg:	What have you done?
Jim:	Let's all calm down.
Gwen:	Sacrificed! Gone without. Gone through hardship so what happened to us will never happen to you. So you'll never know what we saw – never, never, never. Never see people losing jobs and never finding another one, never be without a home, never be without enough money for a decent meal, never be afraid that everything will fall apart at any second. Isn't that something, Miss? Tell me? Isn't it?

Jim:	Let's all relax and calm down.
Meg:	I'm sorry.
Jim:	Just sit down nice and quiet.
Meg:	I'm sorry.
Gwen:	Why are you so cruel?
Meg:	I'm sorry.
Gwen:	Now my head's going to burst. I'm going to take something and then get lunch. *(she goes)*

Stagecraft

Appreciating and performing drama:
Play reading and discussion

Perform a group reading of this scene from *Away*.

This scene contains all the elements of drama. The best way to keep members of an audience entertained and glued to their seats is to present a *conflict*. Where is the conflict in this scene?

For a play to work, the audience must be interested in the *characters*. Discuss the characters of Gwen, Jim and Meg. What have you learnt about them? Are we interested in them, and, if so, why?

A good playwright will tease the audience with a number of *complications* to the plot. These slow down the movement of the play and create suspense. Discuss the complications in this scene. Do they work?

Dramatic action must move towards a *climax*. This is what the audience has been waiting for. Where does the climax come in this scene?

The final stage in the drama is the resolution. Discuss the *resolution* in this scene.

This short scene mirrors the structure of the longer play. It is indeed the structure of the realistic, traditional, well-made play.

Another structure

There is one other structure worth including here. We have already mentioned Brecht, and alluded to his direct way of presenting dialogue.

Bertolt Brecht (1898–1956) was a Marxist who did not want his audience to become emotionally involved when watching plays. He wanted them to think. Consequently, he used techniques to prevent them from losing themselves in the drama. He wanted to remind them that they were only watching a play, and he wanted them to judge what they were witnessing. He wanted them to ask themselves 'Is this right? Is this wrong?'. Techniques used by Brecht to destroy the illusion of theatre include:
- actors speaking to the audience
- actors breaking into song

- actors entering the stage through the audience
- actors playing several roles
- words projected onto screens
- symbolic costume and make-up.

Look at this scene from one of the first scripted Aboriginal plays, *The Cake Man* by Robert Merritt (1974):

Man: *(He opens his eyes and gets groggily to his feet, coughing a little. He discovers a pile of clothes. He picks up a sandshoe and examines it curiously, then another. He tries them out on his hands, then puts them on his feet. He picks up a pair of trousers and experiments with them, trying them on his head and arms before putting them on correctly. A bright red shirt and a cardigan follow. He walks about unsteadily, and it becomes apparent that he is drunk. He looks up and sees the audience for the first time.)* Uh, who you? *(Grinning craftily)* Hey, listen, you wanna buy a boomerang? *(He pulls one from under his coat and holds it up for audience inspection)* Good one, this is. *(Turning it over, reading the back of it)* Made in Japan *(with a grin)* by our trading allies. *(Tossing the boomerang off-stage)* There! Now you seen an Abo throw a boomerang. The Australian champeen is a whitefeller now, it's a fact. A gubba never had a social welfare cheque in his whole life. 'Gubba', that's Kuri lingo for whitefeller. Gubbaahhh is how y'say it if ever y'overseas tellin' someone. I heerd some people in other places is curious about Kuris, an' about our lingo. I know a bit of it, different words an' that. Just ask me an' I'll tell ya. *(Posing proudly now)* See'n I'm a Kuri. The Australian Aborigine, that's who I am and what I am ... made in England.

Hard Times, Ensemble Theatre.

What does Merritt want his audience to think about here?

Today these Brechtian techniques are an accepted part of theatre. As a playwright, you should decide whether you wish to use them or not, and whether they suit your particular presentation.

Notes

Evaluating dialogue (page 163)

1. In the first piece of dialogue, the characters become attitudes rather than people: the exciting young girl and the boring older man. Do not let your characters turn into caricatures.

    People do not usually go around spouting their philosophies. People live out their philosophies rather than preaching them. Avoid preachy lines.

    Successful dialogue needs conflict. This conflict is ineffective as it is unbalanced. The girl gets all the strong lines.

2. The second piece of dialogue comes from *All My Sons* by Arthur Miller. In this play the father made faulty engine parts for aeroplanes during the war, though not purposefully. He didn't tell anybody. He needed the business, which he built up for his sons. One of his sons crashed while flying. The other found out about the faulty heads, and in this scene he confronts his father with the discovery.

    The strong plot creates the drama here. These characters reveal themselves by talking about something else.

    This piece also contains well-developed characters, and an argument that has some balance to it. Although the son takes the high moral ground, it is still possible to understand the father's point of view. Notice how the repetition of words and phrases also intensifies the drama.

3. The third excerpt has all the stage directions written into it. People don't go around giving a running commentary on their own actions. If the audience can see a thing happening on stage, they don't need to be told about it as well.

    A play should consist only of words that *have to be said*; words that have been forced out of the characters.

    Prune your work endlessly.

Unit assessment

Making drama: Writing your own scene

(Six to eight lessons' preparation.)

It is time for you to write a scene of your own. You should aim to write about eight to twelve pages. It is estimated that a typed page of dialogue runs for about two minutes on the stage.

- Start with a diagram of your stage setting.
- Include a character list.
- Write only one scene.
- Edit your work carefully.
- Give your piece a title.
- Present your work neatly typed and with double spacing.

In your logbook

- Keep lesson-by-lesson entries, recording your process.
- Afterwards, include a self-assessment evaluating the success of scripting the scene.

Assessment criteria

- Knowledge and understanding of the elements of scriptwriting
- Ability to control the dynamics of a scripted scene
- Ability to rework a script
- Analysis of the process, and self-evaluation

Assessment feedback sheet

Writing your own scene

	Level of Achievement		
	Developing	Substantial	Excellent

Performance

Knowledge and understanding of the elements of scriptwriting	1	2	3	4	5
Ability to control the dynamics of a scripted scene	1	2	3	4	5
Ability to rework a script	1	2	3	4	5
Expertise in writing dialogue	1	2	3	4	5

Logbook

Recording of your process	1	2	3	4	5
Analysis of the process, and self-evaluation	1	2	3	4	5

Teacher's comments

_____
_____
_____
_____
_____
_____
_____

Student's comments on their strengths, as well as areas that need more work, thought and attention

_____
_____
_____
_____
_____
_____
_____
_____

Commonly used theatrical terms

Accept To say yes to an offer in improvisation.

Acoustics The quality of sound in any particular theatre space.

Ad lib Improvising or adding some lines which are not in the original script.

Advance To contribute a new idea to help an improvisation move forward.

Apron stage A square of stage which juts out into the audience — also known as a thrust stage.

Arena stage A round stage, usually with the audience raised up all around it, in the style of the early Greek theatres.

Aside A remark made by a character on stage, directly to the audience, which the other stage characters are not supposed to hear.

Audition A 'hearing' in which actors competing for a stage role perform for the director.

Auditorium The area in the theatre where the audience sits.

Backcloth A painted canvas at the back of the stage which forms part of the set.

Backstage The area behind the stage, including wings, dressing rooms, and so on.

Bit part A small role with few or no words.

Black comedy A type of play that provokes laughter about a gruesome subject.

Blackout A sudden cut of the stage lights to achieve a dramatic effect.

Blacks Black pants and tee-shirts worn by actors. This neutral costuming focuses attention on the acting rather than the costumes, particularly in workshop situations.

Block To respond negatively in improvisation.

Blocking The movement of characters on stage during a scene. Blocking plans are usually devised by a director.

Box set A realistic stage set built like a box. These sets are usually constructed on a proscenium arch stage.

Bump in The process of carrying in a set and constructing it in a theatre.

Bump out The striking or taking down of a stage set.

Burle Comic routines in *Commedia dell'Arte* between two characters.

Business A term used in melodrama to indicate stage action not described in the stage directions.

Cabaret A late-night entertainment in clubs or restaurants, consisting of songs, dances and short sketches.

Call The request for an actor to leave their dressing room and prepare to go on stage.

Catharsis The purifying moment in theatre when the audience feels cleansed as a result of its emotional involvement in the play.

Characterisation The ability of an actor to adopt the mannerisms, gestures and motivations of another person.

Chorus A group of actors who may sing, dance or speak in unison.

Collage playbuilding The process of exploring a theme, issue or story by assembling theatrical fragments and presenting them in performance.

Comedy A play designed to make the audience laugh.

Commedia dell'Arte A form of improvisational theatre in which actors play stock characters, perform comedy routines (called *lazzi*), and use masks over the top half of their faces. This form of theatre developed in Italy around the sixteenth century.

Compere A master of ceremonies who introduces the acts in a variety show.

Concetti Comic monologues used in *Commedia dell'Arte* to provide a break in the action, allowing the performers to exhibit their skills.

Cue The line, or piece of stage business, in a play which immediately precedes your line, entrance or move.

Designer The person responsible for the visual appearance of the show. This includes the lighting, set, costumes and make-up.

Deus ex machina A contrived ending, relying more on coincidence and orchestration than logical development. The original 'god out of a machine' was a device from early Greek theatre, where a god literally descended from above the stage to solve any problems of plot, and conclude the drama.

Director The person responsible for the style and interpretation of a script.

Downstage The part of the stage nearest the audience.

Duologue A conversation between two people on stage.

Elements of drama The fundamental building blocks of drama.

Epic theatre A play in which a series of episodic scenes are strung together, often with a didactic purpose. This term is usually associated with the playwright Bertold Brecht (1898–1956), who used large casts and non-naturalistic techniques. For example, his cast members might burst into song or talk directly to the audience.

Exposition The introduction of the characters and basic plot of a play to the audience by the playwright in the early lines of a script.

Extend To develop and explore an offer in improvisation.

Farce A style of theatre where events are exaggerated beyond the bounds of reality for comic effect.

Flat A piece of scenery consisting of painted canvas stretched over a wooden frame.

Flies The space above the stage where scenery can be 'flown' when not in use — also known as the flytower.

Focus The point on the stage where the audience's attention should be directed at any given moment during a play.

Fourth wall This refers to the proscenium arch, which would be the 'fourth wall' of a realistic box set. The wall has been removed, however, to allow the audience to see the play.

Front of house The area of the theatre at the front of the stage, consisting of the auditorium, the foyer, ticket collection, ushers.

Gels Coloured filters placed in the lanterns to create specific on-stage moods.

Gobo A metal slide which throws a sharp-edged outline of a picture onto a backcloth.

Houselights Lights in the auditorium.

Impro/Improvisation The acting out of a scene or story without the use of a written script.

Issue-based playbuilding The process of exploring political or social themes and concerns, and presenting them in performance.

Kitchen-sink drama Modern plays set in sordid surroundings and dealing with working class life.

Lanterns Stage lights.

Lazzi Humorous routines in *Commedia dell'Arte* — inserted for comic relief.

Logbook A book in which drama students record the progress of their work.

Magic 'as if' A technique used by Stanislavski (1863–1938) to help the actor believe in their character and the situation.

Mannerisms The small physical movements and gestures that are characteristic of individual people.

Masking One actor obscuring the audience's view of another actor.

Melodrama Literally, 'drama with music'. The type of play where plots are predictable, characters are stereotypes, and good overcomes evil.

Method acting A style of acting developed by Stanislavski which explores the inner motivation for every move and action.

Mime A style of performance that uses gesture, movement and facial expression, but no dialogue.

Monologue An uninterrupted speech made by one character, usually alone on stage.

Morality play A type of play with a strong Christian message which developed in medieval times.

Motivation The reason why a character behaves in a particular way.

Music hall A type of theatre which became popular in the nineteenth century, which involves music, colourful costumes and visual effects.

Narrative playbuilding The process of using the elements of drama to present a story for an audience.

Naturalistic Theatre which reflects the realistic details of everyday life.

Notes Comments made by a director to the actors after a performance.

Offer Anything that is done to stimulate a response in improvisation.

Open stage A stage which is not restricted by a proscenium arch. An open stage could be a thrust stage, an arena stage or a theatre-in-the-round arrangement.

Pace The speed with which lines are delivered.

Pageant A large-scale open-air spectacle, often consisting of a series of scenes re-enacted from history.

Pantomime A popular form of entertainment, consisting of song, dance and music hall acts, and based loosely around a well-known fairy tale.

Planned improvisation An improvisation acted out after some brief planning.

Playbuilding The process of creating an original piece of drama/theatre.

Pre-text The actions and emotions that a stage character might have experienced immediately before coming on stage in a particular scene.

Projection The ability of actors to make themselves heard without shouting.

Prompt The supplying of an actor during rehearsal with the words that they have forgotten.

Props Objects used by actors on stage.

Proscenium arch stage A conventional picture-frame stage where the curtains are opened to reveal the set, and are usually drawn again between acts. Today this is considered a rather restrictive type of staging.

Protagonist The central character in the drama.

Raked stage A stage which slopes gently upwards away from the audience.

Rehearsal The process the director and cast go through in preparing their performance.

Repertoire A group of plays.

Revolving stage A circular section of the stage flooring that can rotate to enable the changing of sets.

Revue A comic or satirical performance made up of separate acts of song, dance and entertaining routines.

Rostrums Portable platforms that can be used to create different levels of staging.

Scene A section of a play.

Script The written text of a play.

Set The scenery and furniture that make up the setting for the play.

Sightlines These are imaginary lines drawn from the stage to the audience. Anyone in the audience sitting outside the sightlines would not be able to see the play.

Simultaneous set A stage construction consisting of several sets on the stage at the same time.

Slapstick Two thin pieces of wood bound together which make a great deal of noise when one comedian beats another with it.

Snap Bringing the lights on quickly.

Soliloquy A monologue spoken by a character alone on stage.

Spotlight A bright moveable light which can be projected onto a lead actor and follow them around the stage.

Stage-left The left side of the stage as experienced by the actor. Thus, it is the right side of the stage if you take the audience's point of view. This is also the Prompt Side (PS) of the stage.

Stage-right The right side of the stage as experienced by the actor. Thus, it is the left side of the stage if you take the audience's point of view. This is also the Opposite Prompt side (OP) of the stage.

Stand-by table A table which stands in the wings, and from which hand props can be picked up by actors before going on stage, and to which they are returned when the actor exits the stage.

Stereotype A caricature; someone who possesses the characteristics of an easily recognisable individual.

Strike To remove a prop or object from the stage.

Subtext The communication that takes place between characters — irrespective of the words spoken.

Tableau A frozen stage picture — usually used at the end of an act in melodrama to create a theatrical climax.

Tabs Curtains.

Taking stage A call for actors to play a scene, moving around the stage freely, creating their own staging as they go, with no direction from the director.

Theatre of the Absurd A type of theatre which began with the works of Ionesco, Beckett and Pinter in the 1950s, and which reflects a world of menace and unexplained human behaviour where human beings fail to communicate. Plays of this kind can be frightening or very funny. In these plays our existence is seen as being without purpose; in a word: absurd.

Theatre-in-the-round A configuration for a play where the audience sits all around the stage area.

Thespian An actor, named after Thespis, supposedly the first actor in Greek theatre.

Three-scene A scene acted out by three characters.

Through line The continuity of similar objectives that a character may have which run through a series of speeches.

Throw-away A line which is deliberately underplayed for a particular dramatic effect.

Thrust stage A square of stage that juts out into the audience, also known as an apron stage.

Timing The ability of an actor to deliver a line at a time when it will have maximum dramatic effect.

Tragedy A play which deals with a heroic person brought to a sad and humiliating end, often as a result of their own actions.

Two-scene A scene acted out by two characters.

Understudy An actor who studies a role and is prepared to step into the part if the lead player is unable to perform.

Unit set A single set that is basic to the whole play.

Upstage The part of the stage furthest from the audience.

Upstaging A process whereby one actor pulls the audience's attention away from where it should be, and on to themselves instead.

Vaudeville A style of theatre which developed in the 1920s consisting of song, dance, circus skills and comedy routines.

Wings The backstage area at the sides of the stage. Actors waiting in the wings to make their entrances cannot be seen by the audience.

Workshops Practical drama sessions which may be used for drama exercises, games or rehearsals for plays. Workshops are usually not carried out in the theatre but in some other available space.

Zanni The primary comic characters in *Commedia dell'Arte*.

Index

action, 24, 31, 46, 114, 117, 128, 142
    dramatic, 167, 169, 180

After Dinner, 125–8

All My Sons, 182

All Stops Out, 116–17, 152–3, 121

animals, 64, 67, 174

Aristophanes, 30

asides, 96

atmosphere, 10, 11, 45

attitudes, 8, 16, 76, 122

audience, 30, 31, 32, 48, 94, 140, 154, 175, 177
    addressing the, 171, 180
    Commedia, 58, 59, 60, 66, 68, 69
    engagement, 10–11, 52, 148
    awareness of the, 156
    expectation, 143
    involvement, 48, 147
    melodrama, 86, 89, 103
    reaction, 45, 155–6

Australian Melodrama, 104

Away, 177–80

Berkley, Bubs, 105

blocking, 128,
    in improvisation, 5, 128
    options for, 153
    a script, 131

Boal, Augusto, 48

body language, 6, 9, 19, 64, 67, 68
    in melodrama, 93
    see also mime
    see also movement

brainstorming, 44, 49

breathing, 92, 120, 149, 155, 172
    see also exercises

Brecht, Bertolt, 48, 170, 171, 180, 181
    epic theatre, 48

burle, 59, 75–6

business, 69, 114
    props, 153
    stage, 153

The Cake Man, 181

caricature, 166, 182
    see also stock characters
    see also stereotypes

carnival, 58, 80

character, 9
    clearly drawn, 145
    finding, 170
    history, 39, 134
    list, 36, 114
    models, 136
    profile, 39, 135
    revealed through action, 117
    revealed through dialogue, 116
    revealed though relationships, 122
    revealed through response, 118
    research, 64, 133
    types, 15

charades, 6

chorus, 170

cliched dialogue, 162, 166–7

climax, 34, 92, 101, 115, 116, 180

clown, 48, 58, 61

Coelina, ou l'enfant du mystère, 96

collaboration, 26, 39, 43
see also groups, working in

collage playbuilding, 43–6

comedy, 20, 52, 58
burle, 76
farce, 48, 52, 104
grotesque, 48
improvised, 58
in Commedia, 64, 70
Kath and Kim, 76
Laurel and Hardy, 76
pantomime, 52, 58
parody, 60
satire, 34, 48
slapstick, 48, 70
using music, 101
see also laughter

Commedia dell'Arte, 58–82
acting style, 68
An Actor's Handbook, by John Rudlin, 64
animals, 64, 67
Arlecchino, 59, 64, 77
audience, 58, 59, 60, 66, 68, 69
Brighella, 59
burle, 59, 75
Colombina, 59, 64, 77
concetti, 59, 75
contradictory action, 70
costume, 60
elements of, 59
Flavio, 59, 64
Il Capitano, 59, 64, 77
Il Dottore, 59, 64
Isabella, 59, 64
lazzi, 59, 70, 72
mask, 64, 65, 72, 67, 68
origins, 58
Pantalone, 59, 64
Pedrolino, 59, 64
plot, 77
props, 61
scenarios, 59, 82
Soubrette, 86, 91
stage, 80, 81
stock characters, 59, 60
zanni, 60, 61, 64,

concentration, 71, 72, 149, 155, 156
see also focus

conflict, 9, 21, 22, 34, 116, 180, 182
dramatic elements of, 9, 21
exploring, 21
identifying, 143, 157
in melodrama, 93
in monologues, 142
interpersonal conflict, 33

content
in melodrama, 103
in playbuilding, 30
in scripted drama, 147

conventions, 148
audience, 104
dramatic, 30
of melodrama, 103

coping
with audience reaction, 155
with nerves, 155
with other actors, 136

costume, 32, 40, 52, 137, 170, 181
in Commedia, 60
in melodrama, 91

dance, 46, 52, 59, 80

deus ex machina, 172

devices,
dramatic and theatrical, 37, 44, 50

dialogue, 114, 115
cliched, 162, 166–7
evaluating, 163, 182
finding a character from, 116
flow, 174, 175
games for developing, 173
learning, 132, 152
writing, 164–5

director, 39, 40, 59, 132, 150, 176

A Doctor in Spite of Himself, 164–5

A Doll's House, 48, 115

drama
elements of, 9, 114
medieval, 30, 96
scripted, see script

dramatic
action, 167

meaning, 9, 30
tension, 9, 10, 17

East Lynne, 88

Elizabethan drama, 96

endings, 172

Entertaining Mr Sloane, 144, 157

entrances and exits, 24, 40, 73, 81, 114, 130–1, 137, 171, 173, 181

exercises
   alphabet mime, 14
   alphabet without the vowels, 152
   applause, 72
   'bank, river, boat', 149
   before and after, 121
   breakfast (*Commedia*), 71
   breakfast mime (concentration), 24
   breath, 92
   bus stop, 173
   communicate without words, 92
   confusion bingo, 66
   distractions, 152
   freeze-frames, 92
   a group of ..., 130
   hiding the lines, 173
   hot seat, 121
   I went shopping, 152
   I'll have the usual, 24
   impaired speech, 121
   magic 'as if', 148
   Mexican wave, 92
   the mirror, 149
   move as ..., 130
   'movie, song, book', 152
   opposites, 14
   power-play improvisations, 173
   relaxation, 120, 172
   remote control, 23
   seconds delay, 71
   show me ..., 7
   slo-mo spine roll, 92
   soap box, 71
   space-jump, 7
   supermarket mime, 8
   tongue twisters, 121
   TV guide, 14
   walk the walk, 72

   welfare agency, 18
   what are you doing?, 23
   writing stage dialogue, 165
   wrong number, 173

exposition, 170, 171

facial expression, 24, 67
   see also body language

film, 34, 86, 102, 115, 145, 168, 169

Fo, Dario, 48

focus, 9, 20, 52, 120, 155

games, *see* exercises

gestures, 6, 59, 64, 68, 86, 130
   in melodrama, 89, 93

Greek drama, 96

Greeks, the, 170, 172

group scenes, 134

groups,
   working in, 7, 8, 9, 17, 33, 37

grummelot, 67

A Hard God, 146

hero, 30, 86, 96, 105, 172

heroine, 30, 86, 96, 105

Ibsen, Henrik, 48, 115, 171

imagination, 4, 43, 81

improvisation, 4–8
   accept, 5
   advance, 5
   block, 5
   burle, 76
   extend, 5
   from mime and movement, 25
   from newspaper headlines, 15
   how to improvise, 6
   offer, 5
   planned, 22–3, 26
   spontaneous, 11
   techniques, 6, 14
   with characters, 15
   see also exercises

inspiration, 12, 46, 52, 133, 169

issue-based playbuilding, 48–52

jump, lateral, 52

Kath and Kim, 76

The Keepers, 144

Lady Audley's Secret, 96–101

language, 9, 48, 116, 117, 140, 145, 166

The Last Two People on Earth, 118–20

laughter, 80, 156
   see also comedy

Laurel and Hardy, 76

Leunig, Michael, 12, 13, 14

lighting, 32
   in epic theatre, 48
   in melodrama, 91, 95

location, 36
   see also setting

Lysistrata, 30

make-believe, 4

make-up, 52, 60, 64, 181
   in melodrama, 91
   see also masks

masks, 60, 64, 65, 67, 72, 73

medieval drama, 30, 96

melodrama, 30, 86–111
   acting style, 89
   audience, 103
   Australian, 104
   elements of, 86
   lighting, 91, 95
   origins of, 104
   plays, 96
   staging, 102
   stock characters, 86
   tableaux, 88, 92, 102
   theatres, 94

Merritt, Robert, 181

message, 30, 31, 32, 48

Miller, Arthur, 182

mime, 7, 14, 24, 46, 52, 71, 72
   alphabet mime, 14
   breakfast mime, 24
   supermarket mime, 8

mirror, 72, 149

Mixed Doubles, 148

Molière, 58, 77, 79, 164, 165

moment, 11, 14, 39

monologues, 140–57
   characterisation, 145
   choosing a monologue, 140
   conflict, 142
   content, 147
   elements, 140
   the magic 'as if', 148
   the performance, 154
   performing a monologue, 147
   using references, 151

mood, 24, 45, 164, 165, 72

morality plays, 30, 96

mountebank, 58

movement, 9, 10, 24, 25, 40, 64, 128, 130
   in *Commedia*, 72
   in melodrama, 89, 93

movies, *see* film

music, 46, 52, 70, 80
   in melodrama, 86–8, 96, 102
   see also song
   see also sound

mystery, 17

narrative playbuilding, 34–41

nerves, 40, 155

newspapers, 26–7, 34, 35, 48
   headlines, 15
   for inspiration, 169, 170

notes, 132
   scripted drama, monologues, 157, 181
   evaluating dialogue, 181

novels, 34, 97, 114

objectives, 21, 33, 117, 125, 128, 136, 145, 157, 173

opposites, 14, 69

pantomime, 52, 58

paradox, 69, 172

period, 9, 11
   see also setting

Pixerecourt, 96

place, 9, 10, 12, 34, 130
   see also setting
   see also location

playbuilding, 30–53
   collage, 43–6
   issued-based, 48–52
   narrative, 34–41
   productive sessions, 38
   unproductive sessions, 39

playreading, 114
   Away, 180
   A Doctor in Spite of Himself, 164
   Lady Audley's Secret, 97
   The Sunny South, 105

plot, 34, 46, 116, 164, 170
   advancing the, 167
   finding a, 169
   in melodrama, 86
   in monologues, 142
   see also story

poetry, 23, 34, 43

politics, 43, 48

pressure, 16
   see also nerves

props, 24, 40, 48, 76, 137, 153
   in *Commedia*, 61

proverbs, 31

PS Your Cat is Dead, 150

purpose, 21
   see also objective
   see also conflict

references, 151–2

rehearsal, 26, 40, 132, 134, 136, 155, 172, 174

relaxation, 120, 155, 172

research, 37, 45, 51, 64, 133, 134

resolution, 34, 172, 180

Restoration drama, 133

rhythm, 8, 10, 11, 20, 44, 166

role, 9, 16–18

Royal Victoria Theatre, Sydney, 104

satire, 34, 48

scenarios, 24, 73, 77, 82

scene, 168
   starters, 153
   structuring a, 177
   working on a, 38

script
   blocking a, 128
   book, 132, 133
   character history in, 134
   choosing a, 114
   elements of film and television scripts, 115
   group scenes, 124
   play or film script? 115
   reading scripts, 114
   revealed though relationships, 122–3
   revealed through action, 117
   revealed through dialogue, 116
   revealed through response, 118
   two-character scenes, 116

scriptwriting, 161–82
   cliches, 166
   dialogue flow, 174, 175
   drama script, 162
   dramatic action, 167
   evaluating dialogue, 164
   experiments in exposition, 171
   finding a plot, 169
   finding characters, 170
   indirect approach, 164
   short dialogue exercises, 165

sets, 40, 48, 175
   description, 97, 114
   see also stage settings

setting, 9, 170, 175

Shakespeare, William, 30, 46, 58, 166, 170, 171

shot, 168
see also film

sightlines, 128, 129, 175

Simpson, J. 202, 140, 170

situation, 9, 10, 22, 116, 118

slapstick, 48, 61

soap opera, 14

song, 23, 34, 80, 180
see also music

sound, 10, 11, 40
effects, 46, 52
see also music
see also song

space, 9, 10, 20, 51

spine, 32
finding a spine, collage playbuilding, 45
finding a spine, issued-based playbuilding, 51
finding a spine, narrative playbuilding, 37

stage
Commedia, 80–1
configurations, 94, 129
dialogue, 162, 163, 166, 174
directions, 97, 114, 176, 182
entrances, 81, 130–1
limitations, 168
manager, 137
movement, justifying, 130
settings, 39, 40, 86, 175, 176
sightlines, 128, 129, 175

status, 9, 19–20
exploring status, 19
in *Commedia,* 60
recording status, 20
reversing status, 21

stereotypes, 33, 59, 86, 115

stimulus material, 46

stock characters, 59, 86, 91

story, 25, 34, 36, 114, 116, 169, 177
see also plot

stress, 136
see also nerves

structure, 10, 37

The Sunny South, 104–10

suspense, 180

symbolic, 31, 52
costumes and make-up, 181
sets and props, 48

symbols, 10, 11, 43

tableaux, 88, 92, 102

A Tale of Mystery, 96

team work, 7, 34
see also groups, working in

television, 14, 30, 31, 34, 46, 76, 86, 115, 145, 168, 169, 170

That Scoundrel Scapin, 77, 80

theatre manager, 59, 103

Theatre of the Oppressed, 48

theatres, 94–5, 103

time, 9, 11, 12, 34
see also period

timing, 156

tongue twisters, 121, 174

topical allusions, 71, 80, 174

Two Weeks with the Queen, 123–4, 131

values, 16, 21

villain, 30, 86, 96, 105

voice, 80, 93, 115, 121, 130, 166
moving the, 149

warm-up, 6, 9, 14, 23, 40, 66, 92, 102, 120, 130, 149, 152, 155
see also exercises

Acknowledgements

The authors would like to thank Michael Leunig for the use of his cartoons. They would also like to thank the Sydney Theatre Company, Ensemble Theatre, Belvoir Street Theatre Company B, Ensemble Studios, The Rep, Chalkdust Theatre and Everyman Theatre for the use of their production photographs. Finally, they would like to thank the students of The Hills Grammar School for the pictures from their varied school productions, and Liz Pellinkhof as the photographer.

Cover image: Company B Belvoir/Black Swan Theatre's production of *Cloudstreet*. Adapted by Nick Enright and Justin Mojo from the novel by Tim Winton. Directed by Neil Armfield. Photo: Daniel Wyllie as Fish Lamb and Chris Pitman as Quick Lamb. Photo by Heidrum Löhr.

Images: Page 10: Company B Belvoir/Black Swan Theatre's production of *Cloudstreet*. Adapted by Nick Enright and Justin Mojo from the novel by Tim Winton. Directed by Neil Armfield. Photo: Daniel Wyllie as Fish Lamb and Chris Pitman as Quick Lamb. Photography by Heidrum Löhr; **13** (top): © Michael Leunig; **13** (bottom), **14**: Michael Leunig *Strange Creature* Penguin, 2003; **35**: © AP Photo/Joseph Kaczmarek; **43**: Photo by Susan Keogh; **58**: 'Mountebank outside Notre Dame with Pedrolino and Arlecchino' (unattributed engraving). Courtesy of John Rudlin; **70**: Jacques Callot 'Cap. Babeo and Cucuba'. Library of Congress, Prints and Photographs Division [LC-USZ62-94283]; **71**: 'Lazzo of the Tooth Extractor' L. Vaccaro *Recueil Fossard* c.1570; **76**: © Sebastian Costanzo/Fairfaxphotos; **80**: Jacques Callot 'Razullo with long stringed instrument and Cucurucu dancing'. Library of Congress, Prints and Photographs Division [LC-USZ62-99309]; **85, 88, 96**: Theatre Museum, London/V&A Images; **87**: Russell Sweeny *Coming Next Week: A Pictorial History of Film Advertising* New York: Castle Books, 1973; **89, 90**: Illustrations by Bernard Partridge in Jerome K. Jerome *Stage-land: curious habits and customs of its inhabitants* London: Chatto & Windus, 1889; **94, 103**: The Victor Glasstone Theatre Collection; **95**: *Illustrated Sydney News* 19 August 1854; **104**: *The Sunny South*, 1 January 1980. Sydney Theatre Company. Photo: Peter Holderness; **115** (bottom), **134, 136, 142, 151, 154, 164, 168, 170, 180**: Ensemble Theatre; **132**: Company B presents *The Underpants*, written by Carl Sternheim, adapted by Steve Martin. Photo (L-R) Arky Michael, Lucy Taylor, Neil Armfield. Courtesy Belvoir St Theatre; **145**: Company B presents *Our Lady of Sligo*, written by Sebastian Barry, directed by Kate Gaul. Photo: Kate Gaul. Courtesy Belvoir St Theatre; **166**: Company B Presents *The Lieutenant of Inishmore* written by Martin McDonagh, directed by Neil Armfield. Photo (L-R) Dan Wyllie, Rita Kalnejais. Courtesy Belvoir St Theatre; **172, 174**: Courtesy Sydney Theatre Company. Photos by Phil Sheather, reproduced with permission.

Text: 'Aisle angst: big trouble in trolley land': © John Huxley. First published in *The Sydney Morning Herald* 15 January 1998.
'Dimples a mother never forgot': Reprinted with permission of The Associated Press.
Extracts reproduced from: *Away* by Michael Gow, *The Cake Man* by Robert Merrit, *Simpson J. 202* by Richard Beynon, *Blackrock* by Nick Enright, *The Keepers* by Bob Maza, *A Hard God* by Peter Kenna, *Barungin* by Jack Davis, *All Stops Out* by Michael Gow, *Two Weeks With The Queen* by Mary Morris, adapted from the novel by Morris Gleitzman, *After Dinner* by Andrew Bovell, published by Currency Press Pty Ltd.
Extracts from *The Entertaining Mr Sloane* by Joe Orton, and 'Countdown' from *Mixed Doubles*, by Alan Ayckbourn, published by Methuen.
Extract from *The State of the Play* by Roger Hall, published by Victoria University Press.
Translations of Molière, 'Les Fourberies de Scapin' and *A Doctor in Spite of Himself* from *Commedia dell'Arte: An Actors Handbook* by John Rudlin, 1994, Routledge
Extract from *PS Your Cat is Dead* by James Kirkwood reproduced by permission of St Martin's Press.
Extract from 'French Fries' in *Talking With* by Jane Martin, published by Samuel French.

Cambridge University Press would like to thank Judith Seeff at the Sydney Theatre Company Archives, Tanya Cawthorne at Belvoir St Theatre and Wendy Peacock at Ensemble Theatre for their kind assistance with production shots.

Every effort has been made to trace and acknowledge copyright. The publishers apologise for any accidental infringement and welcome information that would rectify any error or omission in subsequent editions.